Study Guide and Workbook
to accompany

ANTHROPOLOGY

Ninth Edition

William A. Haviland

Prepared by

M. L. Miranda
University of Nevada, Las Vegas

Harcourt College Publishers

Fort Worth • Philadelphia • San Diego • New York • Orlando • Austin • San Antonio
Toronto • Montreal • London • Sydney • Tokyo

Cover Image: (tl) Tim Hursley/SuperStock; (tr) Patrick N. Lucero/SuperStock; (br) ©Rommel/Masterfile; (bc) SuperStock; (bl) ©Telegraph Colour Library/FPG International; (cl) ©Freeman Patterson/Masterfile

ISBN: 0-15-506800-8

Address for Domestic Orders
Harcourt College Publishers, 6277 Sea Harbor Drive, Orlando, FL 32887-6777
800-782-4479

Address for International Orders
International Customer Service
Harcourt, Inc., 6277 Sea Harbor Drive, Orlando, FL 32887-6777
407-345-3800
(fax) 407-345-4060
(e-mail) hbintl@harcourtbrace.com

Address for Editorial Correspondence
Harcourt College Publishers, 301 Commerce Street, Suite 3700, Fort Worth, TX 76102

Web Site Address
http://www.harcourtcollege.com

Printed in the United States of America

9 0 1 2 3 4 5 6 7 8 2 0 2 9 8 7 6 5 4 3 2

Harcourt College Publishers

Table of Contents

Introduction
Why Should You Use the
Study Guide and Workbook

Your instructor may or may not require the use of this *Study Guide and Workbook* to accompany William Haviland's text, *Anthropology*, Ninth Edition. However, there are some important reasons why you might find it helpful as you begin your study of cultural anthropology.

First of all, using a study guide and workbook along with the main text for the course forces you to simply spend time with the material. You have probably found that when you think you have read an assignment for a course, often you actually can't recall much of what your read. By adding time to your reading for answering review questions, going over key vocabulary, and so on, you fix the information in your memory in a far more thorough manner. The time you spend each day on your study guide and workbooks will help you to spend less time "cramming" for exams later on.

Second, putting things in your own words, as our *Study Guide and Workbook* requires, is the best way to make the subject your own. Education researchers agree that this is a good way to ensure that simple memorization is replaced by true comprehension of information. In addition, the exercises, which encourage you to grasp concepts rather than memorize words, will help you on tests, in which instructors may phrase things in different ways than your textbook author does. Make the book your own; write in it, do the exercises you find useful, and skip the ones you don't. The book was prepared to help you.

Each chapter of the *Study Guide and Workbook* contains several sections. A synopsis of the chapter is followed by an outline of *what you should learn from the chapter*. Then comes a section of *key terms and names* for you to define or identify and a list of *review questions*, which can be answered in a few sentences. *Fill-in-the-blank* sections will serve as further review of the material. (You can later use these pages to study for tests.) Many chapters also contain *exercises* involving constructing charts or locating cultures on maps.

To help you specifically prepare for exams, there are *multiple-choice practice questions, true/false practice questions, practice matching sets, and practice essays*. All of these are excellent ways of preparing for the various kinds of tests your instructor may create.

Hopefully, you will find this book to be a useful complement to William Haviland's textbook *Anthropology*, Ninth Edition. It has been revised numerous times in response to suggestions from faculty and students over the years. The best questions from previous versions of the study guide were kept.

Chapter 1
The Nature of Anthropology

Synopsis

This chapter introduces the discipline of anthropology, the study of humankind everywhere, throughout time. Anthropology seeks to produce useful generalizations about people and their behavior, to arrive at the fullest possible understanding of human diversity, and to understand those things that all human beings have in common. There are two major subfields of anthropology: physical anthropology and cultural anthropology. Physical anthropology focuses on the biological aspects of being human, while cultural anthropology focuses on human beings as members of society. Because of anthropology's holistic perspective, it can contribute substantially to the resolution of human problems.

What you should learn from this chapter

1. Learn how anthropology helps us to better understand ourselves:
   * explore the impulse to find out who we are and where we came from
   * explain how and why the discipline emerged and developed
   * describe anthropology's relationship to the other social sciences
2. Know the subfields of anthropology and understand their purpose and practice:
   * physical anthropology
   * archaeology
   * linguistics
   * ethnology
3. Appreciate how anthropologists conduct their research and the limits on such research.
4. Understand anthropology's relationship to the "hard sciences" and to the humanities:
   * the hypothesis-testing framework
5. Think about some of the ethical issues that confront anthropologists today.

Key Terms

anthropology

physical anthropology

cultural anthropology

forensic anthropology

culture-bound

archaeology

linguistic anthropology

ethnology

ethnography

participant observation

holistic perspective

informants

hypothesis

theory

ethnohistory

fact

Review Questions

1. What are the four subfields of anthropology? How are they related to each other?

2. How does Haviland define "culture"?

3. Distinguish between ethnology and ethnography.

4. Explain in what sense anthropology is a relatively recent product of Western civilization.

5. How does anthropology use the research of many other disciplines?

6. Why are anthropology and sociology closely allied? What sets them apart?

7. Cultural adaptation, development, and evolution are three general concerns of anthropologists. How are they interrelated?

8. Why do archaeologists excavate sites from the historical period when many documents provide information on recent culture?

9. What is the significance of "The Garbage Project"?

10. Why did archaeologists have difficulty in interpreting remains of large Mayan settlements in Central America?

11. With what aspects of language are linguists concerned?

12. Discuss why anthropology is considered the "most liberating of all sciences."

13. Distinguish between the social sciences and the humanities.

14. Discuss how human behavior and biology are inextricably intertwined. Provide examples.

15. Explain why it took so long for a systematic discipline of anthropology to appear.

16. Explain how the work of an anthropological linguist can contribute to our understanding of the human past.

17. Discuss the problems inherent in scientific anthropology.

18. Discuss the ethical problems that could arise in the process of anthropological research.

19. How do linguists aid in our study of the past?

20. Describe the role of the ethnologist, giving an example of the sort of study an ethnologist would produce.

21. What is participant observation? What are its advantages and disadvantages when compared to other social science methods?

22. Define "ethnohistory" and discuss its contributions to historical and ethnographic understanding.

23. Why might it be advisable to do research outside one's own culture prior to studying one's own?

24. What is meant by cross-cultural comparison? What significance does it have?

25. How did the anthropologist on Truk rule out various explanations of the attack on the truck in which he was riding shortly after his arrival in Truk?

26. How did anthropologist Philleo Nash affect the policies of the Roosevelt and Truman administrations?

27. What are the two key elements in the derivation of scientific laws, according to Haviland?

28. Explain the "self-correcting" nature of science, and give an example.

29. What are the limitations of the scientific approach, according to Haviland?

30. What problems are encountered when using the questionnaire for information gathering in ethnographic research?

31. How was anthropologist Sean Collins able to aid in the understanding of exchange relations in rural Peru?

32. What might be accomplished by research into one particular culture?

33. What distinguishes anthropology from the "hard sciences"?

34. Why must anthropologists exercise caution prior to publishing the results of their research?

35. To whom are anthropologists ultimately responsible?

36. How did Laura Nader explain her ethical position with regard to her work on the Zapotec and on U.S. energy research?

37. What is meant by a "global community"?

Fill-in-the-Blank

1. Anthropology is the study of _____ everywhere, throughout time.

2. Anthropology is one of several disciplines in the social and natural sciences that study humans. It differs from other disciplines primarily in its ability to _____ data from many sources.

3. Anthropologists recognize that human behavior has both _____ and social/cultural aspects.

4. Anthropology is divided into four branches, one of _____ anthropology and three of _____ anthropology (archaeology, linguistics, and ethnology).

5. An example of a practical application of physical anthropology is _____ anthropology, in which anthropologists testify in legal situations concerning human skeletal remains.

6. Archaeology is the study of culture based on _____ remains.

7. An in-depth description of a specific culture is called an _____.

8. Comparisons of "housework" show that _____ spend less time on household tasks than Westerners do with all their time-saving gadgets.

9. A tentative explanation of the relation between certain phenomena (e.g., "The light failed to work because the filament was broken") is called a _____.

10. When archaeologists studied the Classic period of Mayan civilization, they assumed that tropical forests occupied by people practicing _____ could not support large population clusters.

11. Ethnohistory is the study of cultures of the recent past through the analysis of _____ materials.

12. Anthropological research is just as likely to be funded by the National Science Foundation as it is by the National Endowment for the _____.

13. Whatever distinctions people may claim for themselves, they are _____, specifically _____, and, as such, they share a common ancestry with others like apes and monkeys.

14. The physical anthropologist applies all the techniques of modern _____ to achieve fuller understanding of human variation and the ways in which it relates to the different environments in which people lived.

Multiple-Choice Practice Questions

1. Anthropology is
   a. the study of Western culture primarily through the analysis of its folklore.
   b. the study of humankind everywhere, throughout time.
   c. the study of nonhuman primates through behavioral analysis.
   d. the study of the species *Homo sapiens* by analyzing its biological but not its cultural dimensions.
   e. the analysis of humankind from the subjective perspective of one group.

2. The systematic study of humans as biological organisms
   a. linguistic anthropology
   b. cultural ecology
   c. cultural anthropology
   d. archaeology
   e. None of the above

3. Anthropology differs from other disciplines that study humans in its ability to _____ data from many sources.
   a. synthesize
   b. eliminate
   c. invent
   d. falsify
   e. fabricate

4. Anthropology is traditionally divided into four branches, one of _____ anthropology and three of _____ anthropology.
   a. cultural/physical
   b. physical/cultural
   c. archaeological/linguistic
   d. ethnological/physical
   e. biological/physical

5. As part of your job, you may study the frequency of blood types in human populations, watch the behavior of monkeys and apes, or dig for early hominid bones from East Africa. You are a/an
   a. ethnologist.
   b. primatologist.
   c. ethnologist.
   d. physical anthropologist.
   e. cultural anthropologist.

6. Theories about the world and reality based on the assumptions and values of one's own culture are
   a. simplistic.
   b. irrational.
   c. culture-bound.
   d. relativistic.
   e. inductive.

7. An archaeologist might attempt to
   a. study material remains to reconstruct past cultures.
   b. study present languages to reconstruct when they diverged from a parent stock.
   c. study garbage to explain contemporary behavior.
   d. All of the above
   e. *a* and *c*

8. An archaeologist studies
   a. potsherds.
   b. paleoecology.
   c. genetic drift.
   d. garbage.
   e. *a, b,* and *d*

9. _____ is that branch of anthropology concerned with humans as biological organisms.
   a. Archaeology
   b. Cultural anthropology
   c. Ethnology
   d. Physical anthropology
   e. Paleontology

10. The focus of anthropology is on both evolution and culture. As such it is able to
    a. address the "nature vs. nurture" question.
    b. address certain ethical issues.
    c. discuss the efficacy of various research methods.
    d. address the qualitative vs. quantitative methods issue.
    e. address the political questions of the day.

11. In-depth descriptive studies of specific cultures are called
    a. ethnologies.
    b. ethnobotanies.
    c. biologies.
    d. ethnographies.
    e. anthropologies.

12. The study of two or more cultures is called a/an
    a. ethnology.
    b. case study.
    c. ethnography.
    d. biography.
    e. ethnohistory.

13. Anthropologists doing fieldwork typically involve themselves in many different
    experiences. They try to investigate not just one aspect of culture (such as the political
    system) but how all aspects relate to each other (for example, how the political system
    fits with economic institutions, religious beliefs, etc.). This approach is called the
    _____ perspective.
    a. holistic
    b. ethnological
    c. sociocultural
    d. sociological
    e. culture-bound

14. Ethnographic fieldwork
    a. is usually associated with the study of wealthy elites.
    b. is usually associated with the study of North American society.
    c. is usually associated with the study of non-Western peoples.
    d. can be applied, with useful results, to the study of North American peoples.
    e. *c* and *d*

15. Ethnographic research on the cultural deprivation theories of the 1960s helped to demonstrate that
   a. minority children are culturally deprived.
   b. cultural deprivation causes lack of achievement in minority children.
   c. the theory that minority children fail to achieve because they are culturally deprived is true.
   d. the theory that minority children fail to achieve because they are culturally deprived is a culture-bound theory.
   e. All of the above except *d*

16. Besides being interested in descriptions of particular cultures, the ethnologist is interested in
   a. teaching food foragers how to use timesaving gadgets.
   b. cross-cultural comparisons.
   c. descriptions of nonhuman species.
   d. promoting Western ways.
   e. providing data to various government agencies to help them suppress certain groups.

17. The goal of science is
   a. to discover the universal principles that govern the workings of the visible world.
   b. to develop explanations of the world that are testable and correctable.
   c. to eliminate the need to use the imagination.
   d. All of the above
   e. *a* and *b*

18. Archaeologists studying the Classic period of Mayan civilization before about 1960 made culture-bound assumptions that the Classic Maya
   a. were more developed than present populations in their forms of agriculture.
   b. were food foragers.
   c. practiced the same slash-and-burn cultivation that people do today and therefore could not have lived in large permanent settlements.
   d. lived in large permanent settlements based on slash-and-burn cultivation.
   e. were industrialists with space-age technology.

19. Questionnaire surveys
   a. enable anthropologists to discover unexpected patterns of behavior.
   b. are never used by anthropologists.
   c. are used by anthropologists to supplement information gained by some other means.
   d. are used only by sociologists.
   e. get at real (vs. ideal) patterns of behavior.

20. Ideally, on which of the following are theories in cultural anthropology based?
    a. intensive fieldwork done in a single society
    b. ethnographies from all over the world so that statements made about culture will be universally applicable
    c. worldwide questionnaire surveys
    d. intuitive thinking about society and culture based on experiences in one's own society
    e. the theories about culture formulated by the people one has studied

21. _____ refers to the study of cultures of the recent past through accounts left by explorers, missionaries, and traders and through analysis of archival materials.
    a. Social change
    b. Ethnohistory
    c. Cross-cultural comparison
    d. Science
    e. Formulation of hypotheses

22. Anthropology studies the language of a culture, its philosophy, and its forms of art. In the process of doing research, ethnographers involve themselves intensively in the lives of those they study, trying to experience culture from their informants' points of view. In this sense anthropology is
    a. scientific.
    b. humanistic.
    c. radical.
    d. conservative.
    e. systematic.

23. In the writing and dissemination of research material the anthropologist has to consider obligations to various entities. Which of the following would NOT be one of the groups the anthropologist would be obligated to?
    a. the profession of anthropology
    b. the people who funded the study
    c. the people studied
    d. the anthropologist's parents
    e. None of the above

24. Linguistic anthropology is concerned with
    a. the description of language.
    b. the history of language.
    c. how language reflects a people's understanding of the world around them.
    d. *a* and *b*
    e. *a, b,* and *c*

25. Throughout most of their history people relied on _____ for answers to questions about who they are, where they came from, and why they act as they do.
    a. myth
    b. careful observation
    c. systematic testing of data
    d. folklore
    e. *a* and *d*

26. By scientifically approaching how people live, anthropologists have learned a great deal about both human
    a. frailties and strengths.
    b. instincts and behavior.
    c. differences and similarities.
    d. insensitivity and callousness.
    e. sensitivity and warmth.

27. It was not until the late _____ century that a significant number of Europeans considered the behavior of others different from them to be at all relevant to an understanding of themselves.
    a. nineteenth
    b. twentieth
    c. seventeenth
    d. fourteenth
    e. eighteenth

28. As _____ of data anthropologists are well prepared to understand the findings of other disciplines.
    a. organizers
    b. synthesizers
    c. analyzers
    d. legitimizers
    e. gatherers

29. Another name for physical anthropology is
    a. primatology.
    b. evolutionary biology.
    c. bioecology.
    d. biological anthropology.
    e. forensic anthropology.

30. Although humans are all members of a single species, we differ from each other in some obvious and not so obvious ways. Which of the following would be ways that humans differ?
    a. skin color
    b. the shape of various physical features
    c. biochemical factors
    d. susceptibility to certain diseases
    e. All of the above

31. According to Haviland, we may think of culture as the often unconscious standards by which groups of people operate. These standards are
    a. genetically transmitted.
    b. biologically inherited.
    c. learned.
    d. absorbed by osmosis.
    e. None of the above

32. Another name for sociocultural anthropology is
    a. ethnology.
    b. ethnography.
    c. cultural ecology.
    d. all of the above
    e. None of the above

33. The archaeologist is able to find out about human behavior in the past, far beyond the mere _____ years to which historians are limited, by their dependence upon written records.
    a. 20,000
    b. 10,000
    c. 5,000
    d. 7,000
    e. 8,000

34. Anthropological research techniques are applicable for which of the following research subjects?
    a. the study of non-Western peoples
    b. the study of health-care delivery systems
    c. schools
    d. corporate bureaucracies
    e. All of the above

35. _____ is/are another hallmark of anthropology.
    a. Case studies
    b. Surveys
    c. Random sampling
    d. Cross-cultural comparisons
    e. None of the above

36. In a sense, one may think of _____ as the study of alternative ways of doing things.
    a. participant observation
    b. ethnography
    c. ethnology
    d. case studies
    e. None of the above

37. One well-known forensic anthropologist is
    a. Sheilagh Brooks.
    b. Bernardo Arriaza.
    c. Jennifer Thompson.
    d. Clyde C. Snow.
    e. None of the above

38. From skeletal remains, the forensic anthropologist can NOT establish which of following?
    a. stature
    b. race
    c. sex
    d. marital status
    e. age

39. A pioneering American anthropologist who did work among the Zuni and founded the Women's Anthropological Society in 1885 was
    a. Margaret Mead.
    b. Ruth Benedict.
    c. Martha Knack.
    d. Margaret Lyneis.
    e. Matilda Coxe Stevenson.

40. Through the efforts of _____, many of the great anthropology museums were established.
    a. Franz Boas
    b. Bronislaw Malinowski
    c. John Wesley Powell
    d. Leslie White

41. He established the Bureau of American Ethnology in 1879.
    a. Robert Kroeber
    b. George Peter Murdock
    c. John Wesley Powell
    d. Sean Conlin
    e. Clyde Wood

42. Modern cross-cultural studies in anthropology derive from efforts of this pioneering anthropologist to develop a rigorous methodology.
    a. George Peter Murdock
    b. John Wesley Powell
    c. Sir Edward B. Tylor
    d. Peggy Reeves Sanday
    e. Laura Nader

43. Which of the following services is NOT one that forensic anthropologists are routinely called upon by the police and other authorities to do?
    a. identify potential archaeological sites
    b. identify the remains of murder victims
    c. identify missing persons
    d. identify people who have died in disasters
    e. identify victims of genocide

44. Among the skeletal remains studied by forensic anthropologist Clyde Snow are the remains of
    a. Julius Caesar.
    b. General George A. Custer.
    c. Adolf Hitler.
    d. Josef Mengele.
    e. *b* and *d*

45. This woman anthropologist was hired by the Bureau of American Ethnology in 1888, making her one of the first women in the United States to receive a full-time position in science.
    a. Margaret Mead
    b. Ruth Benedict
    c. Matilda Coxe Stevenson
    d. Laura Nader
    e. Martha Knack

46. _____ and his students made anthropology courses a common part of college and university curricula.
a. John Wesley Powell
b. Fredric Ward Putnam
c. Bronislaw Malinowski
d. Claude Levi-Strauss
e. Franz Boas

47. His classification of Indian languages north of Mexico is still consulted by scholars today.
a. Franz Boas
b. Noam Chomsky
c. Gary Palmer
d. John Wesley Powell
e. George Urioste

48. This woman anthropologist examined a sample of 156 societies drawn from the Human Relations Area File (HRAF) in an attempt to answer such questions as these. Why, and under what circumstances, do men dominate women? Why do women play a more dominant role in some societies than others?
a. Laura Nader
b. Peggy Reeves Sanday
c. A. B. Weiner
d. Ruth Benedict
e. Margaret Mead

Answers to multiple-choice practice questions

1. b	13. a	25. e	37. d
2. e	14. e	26. c	38. d
3. a	15. d	27. e	39. e
4. b	16. b	28. b	40. a
5. d	17. e	29. d	41. c
6. c	18. c	30. e	42. a
7. e	19. c	31. c	43. a
8. e	20. b	32. a	44. e
9. d	21. b	33. c	45. c
10. a	22. b	34. e	46. e
11. d	23. d	35. d	47. d
12. a	24. e	36. c	48. b

True/False Practice Questions

1. Culture is preserved and transmitted by language and observation.

2. While ethnography is the in-depth study of a single culture, ethnology is the comparative study of culture.

3. Ethnographic fieldwork is never done in Western societies.

4. Anthropology can best be defined as the cross-cultural study of social behavior.

5. Forensic anthropologists are particularly interested in the use of anthropological information for the purpose of debate, oratory, and rhetorical criticism.

6. The anthropologist who went to Truk for his fieldwork was killed by a drunken Truk man.

7. A forensic anthropologist can even tell from skeletal remains whether the deceased was right- or left-handed.

8. What a forensic anthropologist cannot tell from skeletal remains are details of an individual's health and nutritional history.

9. Besides providing factual accounts of the fate of victims who had disappeared (*desparecidos*) to their surviving kin, Snow's work helped convict several Argentine military officers of kidnapping, torture, and murder.

10. All cases of forensic anthropologists involve the abuse of police powers, and evidence provided by them is often ancillary to bringing the guilty party to justice.

11. Franz Boas was the first to teach anthropology in the United States.

Answers to true/false practice questions

1. T	4. F	7. T	10. F
2. T	5. F	8. T	11. F
3. F	6. F	9. T	

Practice Matching

Match the disciplines/concepts with their correct description.

1. _____ anthropology

2. _____ physical anthropology

3. _____ cultural anthropology

4. _____ forensic anthropology

5. _____ culture-bound

6. _____ archaeology

a. Field of applied physical anthropology that specializes in the identification of human skeletal remains for legal purposes

b. The systematic study of humans as biological organisms

c. The study of humankind, in all times and places

d. The branch of anthropology that focuses on human behavior

e. The study of material remains, usually from the past, to describe and explain human behavior

f. Theories about the world and reality based on the assumptions and values of one's own culture

Answers to practice matching questions

1. c
2. b

3. d
4. a

5. f
6. e

Practice Essays

1. Illustrate the usefulness of ethnographic fieldwork in North American society by discussing research on the theory of cultural deprivation among minority children.

2. Discuss the characteristics of participant observation and how this method contributes to ethnographic understanding. How is this method characteristically different from other methods of social science research?

3. Describe how anthropology is, at the same time, a social/behavioral science, a natural science, and one of the humanities.

4. It was stated that it has been the office of other social sciences to reassure, while the role of anthropology is to unsettle. Explain what is meant by this.

5. According to the professional code of ethics of the American Anthropological Association, an anthropologist's primary responsibility is to the people he or she studies. Discuss the ethical issues that might arise where there is a conflict of interest between the scholar's commitment to the "truth" and his or her commitment to people.

6. Haviland asserts that anthropology is a kind of testing ground for the cross-cultural validity of disciplines like sociology, psychology, and economics, saying that it is to these disciplines what the laboratory is to physics and chemistry. What theory in another social science discipline can you think of that could usefully be tested cross-culturally?

7. Discuss how the anthropologist in Truk used his experiences with drunken people to explain the cultural dynamics of the society.

8. Your textbook provides a rather lengthy discussion of the difficulties that arise in the application of the scientific approach in anthropology. What are the difficulties that arise when applying the scientific approach in anthropology?

Chapter 2
Methods of Studying the Human Past

Synopsis

Chapter 2 introduces the student to the anthropological study of the past. Distinguishing the fossil from the archaeological record, this chapter outlines methods of site or locality location and excavation. Finally, laboratory analysis and dating techniques are discussed.

What you should learn from this chapter

1. Understand the role of anthropology in studying the past.
2. Know the difference between artifacts and fossils.
3. Understand how sites and localities are located.
4. Understand how sites and localities are excavated.
5. Know the factors affecting the preservation of artifacts and fossils.
6. Understand the process and importance of meticulous recording in archaeological excavation.
7. Describe the various techniques of archaeological dating.

Key Terms

paleoanthropologist

artifact

fossil

unaltered fossil

altered fossil

site

fossil locality

soil marks

grid system

datum point

flotation

stratigraphy

matrix

assemblage

technology

relative dating

absolute (chronometric) dating

fluorine test

palynology

potassium-argon analysis

dendrochronology

amino acid racemization dating

radiocarbon analysis

electron spin resonance

Review Questions

1. Why do anthropologists study the past?

2. What two subfields of anthropology are primarily concerned with studying the past?

3. What is the ultimate goal of archaeology?

4. What does a paleoanthropologist study?

5. What is the ultimate goal of paleoanthroplogy?

6. What do artifacts represent?

7. Why is context important?

8. How might an organism be preserved?

9. Distinguish between altered and unaltered fossils.

10. Describe how a fossil forms.

11. How are archaeological sites discovered?

12. What was discovered at the Windover site in Florida?

13. What two questions should an archaeologist ask herself prior to excavating, according to Haviland?

14. Describe how the grid system is used.

15. How is a fossil excavated?

16. Why and how is plaster of paris put to use in excavation?

17. Of what use is the study of human feces?

18. Describe some factors affecting fossil and artifact preservation.

19. What methods are used in excavation and why are they so meticulous?

20. What can vegetable and animal remains indicate?

21. What can analysis of human skeletal material indicate?

22. Distinguish between relative and absolute (chronometric) dating.

23. What is the basic principle of stratigraphy?

24. List four examples of relative dating.

25. List five examples of chronometric dating.

26. What were the main pieces of legislation in the United States regarding Cultural Resource Management?

Fill-in-the-Blank

1. Human brains preserved in the peat environment at Windover Farms in Florida have yielded the oldest known _____.

2. Stains that show up on the surface of recently plowed fields are called _____.

3. Heinrich Schliemann discovered the ancient city of _____ after reading Homer's *Iliad*.

4. A _____ is the starting or reference point in a grid system.

5. The earth immediately surrounding an artifact or fossil is called the _____.

6. Microscopic wear patterns on teeth can indicate whether _____ were important foods.

7. When carbon 14 disintegrates, it returns to _____.

8. Long-lived trees like _____ are used in dendrochronology.

9. Electron spin resonance measures the number of trapped electrons in _____.

10. Careful record keeping is essential to archaeology because once a site is excavated it is _____.

Exercise

Prepare the following chart, which will summarize the major dating methods used by archaeologists and paleoanthropologists. (Radiocarbon is partially filled in as an example.) You can use this chart to study from later on.

Major Dating Method

Method	Material	Range	Description	Limitations

Multiple-Choice Practice Questions

1. A material object that shows signs of having been made or altered by humans is called a/an
   a. abstract ideal.
   b. relic collector.
   c. artifact.
   d. fossil.
   e. paleoanthropologist.

2. Most fossils have been altered; their organic molecules have been replaced by
   a. metal.
   b. water.
   c. DNA.
   d. calcium carbonate.
   e. ice.

3. Spiders and insects encased in amber; Siberian mammoths frozen in ice; the DNA of 7000-year-old brains found in peat. All of these are examples of
   a. artifacts.
   b. altered fossils.
   c. unaltered fossils.
   d. unaltered artifacts.
   e. commonly found fossils.

4. In which of the following situations is a paleoanthropologist most likely to find the fossil remains of our primate ancestors?
   a. in the middle of the ocean
   b. in tropical forests
   c. on savannas
   d. in the Arctic
   e. on mountaintops exposed to the elements

5. A place that indicates the presence of human occupants in the past (for example, evidence of a temporary hunting camp or more permanent village) is called an archaeological
   a. grid system.
   b. fossil locality.
   c. datum point.
   d. stratigraphic analysis.
   e. site.

6. The term "soil marks" refers to
   a. a place where fossils are found in paleoanthropology.
   b. a system for recording data from an archaeological excavation.
   c. stains that show up on the surface of recently plowed fields, indicating an archaeo-
      logical site.
   d. remains of plants and animals whose organic material has been replaced by silica.
   e. none of the above.

7. The purpose of a grid system is
   a. to record the exact location of an artifact or fossil accurately, both horizontally and
      vertically.
   b. to tell relic collectors where to find artifacts to sell to private collectors.
   c. to provide electricity to primitive villages.
   d. to cook bacon.
   e. to recover small objects immersed in water.

8. Archaeologists and paleoanthropologists share many methods and techniques, but they
   also differ. The following techniques might be learned by both, but which is most
   likely to be associated with the paleoanthropologist?
   a. knowledge of geology
   b. use of a grid system
   c. knowledge of flotation
   d. shovels and trowels
   e. knowing how to drive a jeep

9. Which of the following conditions is most favorable to the preservation of fossils?
   a. a cultural practice in which the deceased is placed on a platform open to predators
      and weather
   b. a wet hillside
   c. burial in volcanic ash
   d. a moist, warm tropical rainforest
   e. a cultural practice in which the deceased is thrown into the mouth of a volcano

10. Archaeologists get clues about how an artifact was used by
    a. coating it with latex.
    b. dissolving it with chemicals.
    c. removing it from its context to look at it without interference from misleading clues.
    d. cutting it into pieces and looking at it under the microscope.
    e. analyzing its shape and signs of wear and tear.

11. A "relative date"
    a. is when you take your cousin out to dinner.
    b. would be represented by the statement, "This fossil is about 100,000 years old, plus or minus 10,000 years."
    c. is the same as a "chronometric date."
    d. would be represented by the statement, "Fossil A has more fluorine in it than Fossil B, so it is the older one."
    e. is based on solar years.

12. Stratigraphy is based on the assumption that layers are deposited in order; thus an artifact or fossil in a lower stratum is _____ one found in a higher stratum.
    a. the same age as
    b. older than
    c. younger than
    d. likely to be descended from
    e. likely to be unrelated to

13. The use of tree rings to assign chronometric dates is called
    a. palynology.
    b. potassium-argon.
    c. dendrochronology.
    d. stratigraphy.
    e. matrix analysis.

14. The half-life of radioactive potassium is
    a. 5,730 years.
    b. 1.3 years.
    c. useful for measuring the age of things as old as 70,000 years.
    d. useful for measuring things millions and billions of years old.
    e. a relative dating method.

15. The radiocarbon method can be used to date organic materials up to _____ years old.
    a. 11,460
    b. 70,000
    c. 5,730
    d. 1.3 billion
    e. 4.5 billion

16. Which of the following is NOT true about the Windover Farms site in Florida?
    a. The artifacts and bones recovered date to more than 7,000 years ago
    b. The culture represented was an early agricultural one
    c. Fabric was recovered clinging to some of the skeletons
    d. Some of the brain tissue was preserved
    e. The site was not fully excavated

17. As mentioned in the original study "Whispers From the Ice," archaeologist
    _____ offered her firm's services to help remove an ancient body found
    in a bluff that had been softened by a rainstorm.
    a. Richard Jensen
    b. Anne Jensen
    c. Richard Leakey
    d. Jennifer Thompson
    e. Ted Goebels

18. The _____, it was pointed out in the original study "Whispers From
    the Ice," agreed to fund the autopsy and subsequent analysis of the body found.
    a. National Endowment for the Humanities
    b. *National Geographic*
    c. National Science Foundation
    d. SJS Archaeological Services, Inc.
    e. The Discovery Channel

19. The point was made in the original study "Whispers From the Ice" that _____
    often know from experience, or from stories, how items were used or made.
    a. young people
    b. elders
    c. archaeologists
    d. museologists
    e. physical anthropologists

20. As stated in the original study "Whispers From the Ice" the early Arctic researchers
    were considered "_____" by some Inupiat Eskimos.
    a. monsters
    b. ghouls
    c. grave robbers
    d. desecrators
    e. morally deficient

21. An analysis of the girl's body, as discussed in the original study "Whispers From the
    Ice," showed that she had _____, which was caused by a diet exclusively of
    meat from marine mammals.
    a. osteoporosis
    b. cancer
    c. tuberculosis
    d. rickets
    e. scurvy

22. The Point Franklin Project, as mentioned in the original study "Whispers From the Ice," did which of the following?
    a. contributed to the knowledge about sea mammal migration
    b. served as a model for proper behavior between Alaskan government officials and archaeologists
    c. contributed to the knowledge of kitchen middens in Arctic environments
    d. provided material for the remake of the movie "Nanook of the North"
    e. served as a model for good relations between archaeologists and Native people

Answers to multiple-choice practice questions

1. c	7. a	13. c	18. c
2. d	8. a	14. d	19. b
3. c	9. c	15. b	20. c
4. c	10. e	16. b	21. a
5. e	11. d	17. b	22. e
6. c	12. b		

True/False Practice Questions

1. Fossils are found in *sites,* while archaeological remains are found in *localities.*

2. Part of the Windover Farm site in Florida was purposely left unexcavated.

3. At Tikal in Guatemala, breadnut trees mark the sites of ancient Maya habitations.

4. In the United States, construction projects that require government approval will not be authorized unless measures are taken to identify and protect archaeological remains that may be there.

5. Human feces unfortunately decay rapidly, so it is impossible to investigate prehistoric diet through excrement.

6. In the United States, federal law requires the return of Native American skeletons for reburial.

Answers to true/false practice questions

1. F	3. T	5. F
2. T	4. T	6. T

Practice Matching

1. dendrochronology

2. potassium-argon

3. palynology

4. electron spin resonance

5. radiocarbon

a. used on volcanic rock

b. used on bone or shell

c. tree-ring dating

d. used on any organic material

e. study of fossil pollen

Answers to practice matching

1. c   2. a   3. e   4. b   5. d

Practice Essays

1. Describe the conditions that may affect the preservation or decay of an organism. What difficulties do paleoanthropologists face when they try to find traces of ancient humans? Why is the discovery of American Indian remains in Florida peat bogs considered especially significant?

2. You are a paleoanthropologist who has just discovered an ancient human-looking skull in East Africa. How would a knowledge of geology help you date it? Describe the techniques you would use to remove and preserve the skull.

3. The findings from the autopsy of the frozen girl's body described in the original study "Whispers From the Ice" suggest what about the girl's life?

Chapter 3
Biology and Evolution

Synopsis

Chapter 3 describes the mechanisms that form the basis of all organisms and that contribute to evolution. The evolutionary forces exerted on populations are explored as are evolutionary processes. Finally, the development of species and controlling factors to species' development are discussed.

What you should learn from this chapter

1. Understand the mechanisms of heredity that enable evolution to occur.
   - DNA
   - genes
   - chromosomes
   - mitosis
   - meiosis
   - alleles
2. Know how evolution works in a population.
   - Hardy-Weinberg Principle
   - mutation
   - genetic drift
   - gene flow
   - natural selection
   - adaptation
3. Understand sickle-cell anemia and its implications for understanding evolution.
4. Be able to differentiate between linear, divergent, and convergent evolution.
5. Understand what a species is and how it evolves.

Key Terms and Names

anthropomorphism

primate order

heredity

gene

DNA

chromosome

allele

mitosis

meiosis

homozygous

heterozygous

phenotype

genotype

hemoglobin

sickle-cell anemia

polygenetic inheritance

population

gene pool

evolution

Hardy-Weinberg Principle

mutation

genetic drift

gene flow

adaptation

natural selection

Charles Darwin

directional selection

stabilizing selection

divergent evolution

convergent evolution

species

races

isolating mechanisms

Review Questions

1. Who pioneered the study of genetics? What were his basic insights?

2. What is meant by the comment that our DNA is "nine-tenths junk"?

3. What is the function of chromosomes and where are they located?

4. Distinguish between mitosis and meiosis.

5. How many chromosomes are present in human cells?

6. Distinguish between homozygous and heterozygous.

7. Distinguish between phenotype and genotype.

8. What are recessive, dominant, and codominant alleles?

9. According to the Hardy-Weinberg Principle (HWP), what four conditions must be met for a population to maintain a stable gene pool?

10. What is an average number of mutant genes in the human population? Why is some amount of mutation considered normal?

11. What external influences may increase the rate of mutations in a population?

12. Give an example of genetic drift and consider its implications for evolution.

13. When does gene flow occur?

14. Differentiate between directional selection and stabilizing selection.

15. Give an example of how biological and cultural evolution are related.

16. What are some adaptive traits exhibited by humans?

17. Where and why did sickle-cell evolve?

18. Why is sickle-cell anemia harmful to North Americans of African descent?

19. What is a major drawback of a species that is too well adapted to its environment?

20. Distinguish between divergent and convergent evolution.

21. Provide three examples of isolating mechanisms.

Fill-in-the-Blank

1. Charles Darwin's landmark book, published in 1859, was _____.

2. _____ is the protein that carries oxygen in the red blood cells.

3. An important modern cause of mutation is _____.

4. _____ is a contemporary scientist interested in the role of chance factors in evolution.

5. The pioneer of modern genetics was the Austrian monk _____.

6. Genetic drift, the effect of chance events on evolution, is particularly significant for _____ populations.

7. DNA was discovered in 1953 by _____.

Exercises

1. Here is a greatly enlarged, two-dimensional model of a DNA molecule. It is called a "double helix" and looks like a twisted ladder. The supports of the ladder are made of alternating sugars and phosphates, and the rungs are made of pairs of bases connected at the center by hydrogen. It is the sequence of base pairs that comprises the "genetic code" for particular traits.

   In this model, color the sugars *red.* Color the phosphates *blue.*

   Now color the base pairs: cytosine and guanine should be *yellow* and *orange* while adenine and thymine should be *purple* and *green.* Note that the adenine always goes with the thymine and the cytosine always goes with the guanine. (This is how DNA halves replicate; they attract the complementary bases.)

   Color the hydrogen bonds *brown.*

   Now, starting from left to right, write down the "genetic code" embedded in this DNA molecule: e.g., TA - GC - CG - CG - . . .

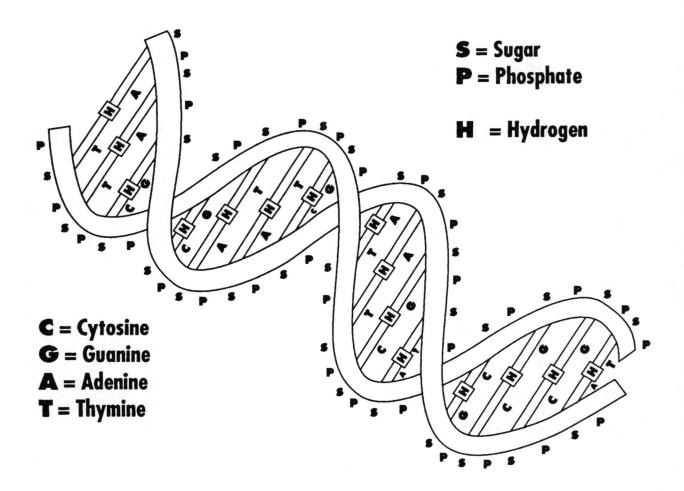

S = Sugar
P = Phosphate

H = Hydrogen

C = Cytosine
G = Guanine
A = Adenine
T = Thymine

2. Use this space to draw the main phases of mitosis and meiosis. Note in words what the end result is of each process.

Multiple-Choice Practice Questions

1. The raw material for evolution is the unit of heredity called the
   a. garden pea.
   b. physical trait.
   c. genetic drift.
   d. gene.
   e. isolating mechanism.

2. What is the relationship between a "gene" and DNA?
   a. A gene is part of the complex molecule called DNA; it is a particular section that contains the code responsible for a particular trait.
   b. A gene is a complete molecule of deoxyribonucleic acid.
   c. A gene is the visible trait created by the actions of DNA.
   d. There is no relationship; the two are parts of different processes.
   e. They are both the same thing.

3. Which of the following statements about chromosomes does NOT apply to chromosomes in humans?
   a. Humans have 23 pairs of chromosomes.
   b. Chromosomes are found in the cell nucleus.
   c. Humans have 46 pairs of chromosomes.
   d. Paired chromosomes may have slightly different versions of the gene for a particular trait.
   e. DNA is combined with protein to form structures called chromosomes.

4. In human mitosis, a cell with 46 chromosomes divides into two new cells, each with 46 chromosomes. In human meiosis, a cell with 46 chromosomes divides into four new cells, each with _____ chromosomes.
   a. 46
   b. 102
   c. 23
   d. 12
   e. 4

5. When you give blood to the Red Cross, you are told that you have Type O blood. You are puzzled, because your mother has Type A blood and your father has Type B blood. If you hadn't taken this class, you might have decided that you were adopted; but now you know that your mother probably has the genotype _____ and your father probably has the genotype _____.
   a. AO/BO
   b. OO/OO
   c. AA/BB
   d. AB/AB
   e. AO/BB

6. A person receives a gene for A type blood from his mother, and a gene for O type blood from his father. His phenotype is A blood. The gene for A type blood can be described as
   a. positive evolution.
   b. adaptive.
   c. a dominant allele.
   d. a recessive allele.
   e. a genotype.

7. Heritable skin color in humans is caused by
   a. a single gene.
   b. two alleles that are codominant.
   c. at least three separate genes (called polygenes).
   d. a recessive gene.
   e. a gene with incomplete dominance.

8. The study of inheritance in individuals tells us about how genes can be combined and recombined through sexual reproduction; but to see how species change over time as natural selection favors some combinations over others, we need to look at
   a. two individuals.
   b. populations.
   c. gene flow.
   d. genetic drift.
   e. directional selection.

9. The Hardy-Weinberg Law is a theoretical model of a population that is
   a. evolving.
   b. not evolving.
   c. undergoing intense pressure to change.
   d. changing from Communism to Capitalism.
   e. migrating from England to Germany.

10. Among the following factors that affect the genetic stability of a gene pool, which is the ultimate source of new genes that are added to the gene pool?
    a. genetic drift
    b. gene flow
    c. mutation
    d. random mating
    e. natural selection

11. Changes in the frequency of genes in a gene pool caused by accidental, random, chance events
    a. is called gene flow.
    b. is called genetic drift.
    c. is more likely to occur in small populations.
    d. *a* and *c*
    e. *b* and *c*

12. The introduction of alleles from the gene pool of one population into that of another is called
    a. mutation.
    b. genetic drift.
    c. gene flow.
    d. natural selection.
    e. convergent evolution.

13. The process by which a population becomes better adapted to its biological and social environment is
    a. natural selection.
    b. mutation.
    c. gene flow.
    d. genetic drift.
    e. meiosis.

14. Despite the usefulness of a large brain in a cultural environment, the size of the human brain has not increased significantly for the last 100,000 years. This is an example of
    a. directional selection.
    b. stabilizing selection.
    c. convergent evolution.
    d. divergent evolution.
    e. isolating mechanism.

15. The case of sickle-cell anemia illustrates that a trait that may bring misery to an individual is adaptive from the point of the view of the
    a. population.
    b. gene.
    c. DNA.
    d. environment.
    e. chromosome.

16. A generalized organism becomes more specialized; one species gradually transforms into a new one; a population becomes increasingly well adapted to its environment. This is _____ evolution.
    a. specialized
    b. divergent
    c. homogenous
    d. linear
    e. spherical

17. Two dissimilar forms develop greater similarities, such as birds and bats. This is an example of
    a. convergent evolution.
    b. divergent evolution.
    c. linear evolution.
    d. genetic drift.
    e. the Hardy-Weinberg Principle.

18. When a single ancestral population gives rise to two or more descendant populations, this is called
    a. convergent evolution.
    b. adaptation.
    c. linear evolution.
    d. stabilizing selection.
    e. divergent evolution.

19. A _____ is a population that is reproductively isolated from other populations.
    a. genotype
    b. phenotype
    c. species
    d. homozygous genotype
    e. heterozygous genotype

20. One theory of the nondirectedness of evolution states that with the demise of the _____, all sorts of evolutionary opportunities became available, and mammals began their great expansion into new niches, including the one in which our own ancestors evolved.
    a. mammoths.
    b. platypus.
    c. saber-toothed tiger.
    d. dinosaur.
    e. Neanderthal

21. Had this essentially random event not happened, or had it happened at some other time, humans would not have evolved and there would probably be no consciously intelligent life on earth.
    a. the Ice Age
    b. the Earth's collision with a comet or asteroid
    c. nuclear holocaust
    d. the Great Flood
    e. El Niño

22. _____ is now widely perceived and appreciated as the organizing principle at all levels of life.
    a. Physics
    b. Natural selection
    c. Quantum physics
    d. Evolution
    e. Social organization

23. Phylogenies are used to track infectious diseases, and they have just been admitted into Louisiana criminal courts to infer _____ transmission.
    a. HIV
    b. *e. coli*
    c. criminality
    d. sickle-cell
    e. cultural

24. _____ exploits the evolution of novel functions in microbes to clean up toxic waste.
    a. Pandemics
    b. Mutation
    c. Recombination
    d. In vitro selection
    e. Bioremediation

Answers to multiple-choice practice questions

1. d	7. c	13. a	19. c
2. a	8. b	14. b	20. d
3. c	9. b	15. a	21. b
4. c	10. c	16. d	22. d
5. a	11. e	17. a	23. a
6. c	12. c	18. e	24. e

True/False Practice Questions

1. The general idea of evolution had in fact been proposed by many writers long before Darwin's time.

2. Stephen Jay Gould has emphasized the nondirectedness of evolution, pointing out that it is not a ladder of progress but a concatenation of improbabilities.

3. Sickle-cell anemia has now been eradicated as a health problem, although scientists continue to study it in the laboratory.

4. Anthropomorphism means the ascription of animal traits to humans.

5. Gregor Mendel discovered many of the founding principles of genetics by studying the garden pea.

Answers to true/false practice questions

| 1.T | 2. T | 3. F | 4. F | 5. T |

Practice Matching

1. isolating mechanism

2. divergent evolution

3. linear evolution

4. species

5. convergent evolution

a. transformation of an old species to a new one

b. a population that is reproductively isolated

c. factors working to separate breeding populations

d. a population gives rise to two or more differing populations

e. organisms develop greater similarities over time

Answers to practice matching

| 1. c | 2. d | 3. a | 4. b | 5. e |

Practice Essays

1. Distinguish between dominant and recessive alleles, using A-B-O blood type to demonstrate the impact that dominance and recessiveness have on phenotype.

2. Distinguish between directional selection and stabilizing selection, and critique the traditional assumption that the evolution of life forms is characterized by steady progress.

3. Explain Stephen Jay Gould's ideas on "the improbabilities of history."

4. According to Haviland, how does cooperative behavior about?

5. In the original study "The Drunkard's Walk," what is the paradigm presented attempting to illustrate?

Chapter 4
Monkeys, Apes, and Humans:
The Modern Primates

Synopsis

Chapter 4 considers humankind in the context of other primates, describing the classification system used to define the primate order as well as the major physical and behavioral characteristics of the primates. The chapter also goes into the evolutionary relationships among the modern primates and explores hypotheses developed to account for the large, complex brains of humans and our emphasis on learning as a major means of adaptation.

What you should learn from this chapter

1. Understand the development and basis of past and present classification systems.
2. Learn the "family tree" of the primates.
3. Understand the characteristics shared by all primates.
   - senses
   - dentition
   - brain
   - reproduction
   - skeleton
3. Know the evolutionary relationships between humans and other primates.
4. Be familiar with the defining features of the various modern primates.
   - Strepsirhines
   - Haplorhines
5. Understand what primatologists have learned of primate social behavior.
   - group behavior
   - individual interaction
   - sexual behavior
   - play
   - communication
   - home ranges
   - learning
   - tool use
   - hunting

Key Terms and Names

analogies

homologies

genus

notochord

Strepsirhini

Lemuriformes

Haplorhini

Tarsii

Platyrrhini

Catarrhini

arboreal

stereoscopic vision

fovea centralis

cranium

foremen magnum

clavicle

scapula

brachiate

pentadactyly

prehensile

estrus

sexual dimorphism

vocalization

home range

tool

Jane Goodall

Review Questions

1. For what purpose was the Linnaean system developed?

2. Distinguish between analogies and homologies.

3. On what three characteristics was Linnaeus' system based?

4. Modern classification systems account for what further characteristics?

5. What are the features that mammals share?

6. Differentiate between the two primate suborders.

7. Over the millennia, what has happened to primates' sense of smell? Touch? Sight?

8. What is stereoscopic vision and why was its development important in evolution?

9. What is the purpose of tactile hairs? Information pads?

10. What three characteristics do all primates' brains share?

11. Why did brain size increase?

12. Why is the development of the hand important in understanding the development of the brain?

13. What role did a larger cortex play in primate development?

14. List four types of mammal teeth and their function.

15. List some prominent changes in primate dentition over the course of evolution.

16. What is the function of the primate skeleton?

17. What accounts for the shape of the primate skull?

18. Why is the position of the foremen magnum important?

19. What occurred as the acuity of the sense of smell declined?

20. Why are primates' arms powerful, maneuverable, and flexible?

21. Why do catarrhines only have a single offspring at a time?

22. Distinguish between Old and New World monkeys.

23. Why do scientists assert that apes are humans' closest relatives?

24. Why are African apes semi-erect?

25. Why do primatologists study the behavior of primates in general and baboons in particular?

26. What are the functions of grooming?

27. Why do baboon mothers often befriend nonkin males?

28. What effect does male chimpanzee wandering have on the structure of chimpanzee groups?

29. Compare and contrast the sexual behavior of chimpanzees and bonobos.

30. What practical functions does play serve?

31. What vocalized messages are used by primates?

32. What are possible explanations of chimpanzee violence on other chimpanzee communities?

33. For what experiment are Japanese macaques known?

34. Differentiate between tool use and tool making.

35. What are some ways that chimpanzees fashion and use tools?

36. To what extent have orangutans been able to learn gestural language?

37. What are the possible explanations of bonobo sexual behavior?

Fill-in-the-Blank

1. Taxonomy is another word for _____.

2. The high level of mammalian activity is made possible by _____.

3. The subfamily _____ is characterized by terrestrial bipedal locomotion and reliance on learned behavior.

4. Most primate adaptations developed in the _____ or tree-dwelling habitat.

5. Three-dimensional or _____ vision was an important factor in primate evolution.

6. Among primates the evolutionary tendency has been for the foremen magnum to shift _____.

7. New World monkeys are characterized by _____ noses.

8. The _____ is the largest of the apes.

9. Chimpanzees live on the continent of _____.

10. _____ use trail markers as a form of communication.

Exercises

1. The following chart summarizes the place of humans in biological classification. Fill in brief *descriptions* of each of the categories we belong to. You can use this to study from later.

The Place of Humans in Biological Classification

KINGDOM	Animals	
PHYLUM	Chordata	
SUBPHYLUM	Vertebrata	
CLASS	Mammalia	
ORDER	Primates	
FAMILY	Hominidae	
SUBFAMILY	Homininae	
GENUS	*Homo*	
SPECIES	*sapiens*	

2. Look at the indri, macaque, gorilla, chimpanzee and human skeletons below. Write down the *similarities* and *differences you* see among them. Note that two key features of humans are their brain size (with corresponding changes in the shape of the skull) and their bipedalism or two-legged stance. What evolutionary factors might have contributed to these developments?

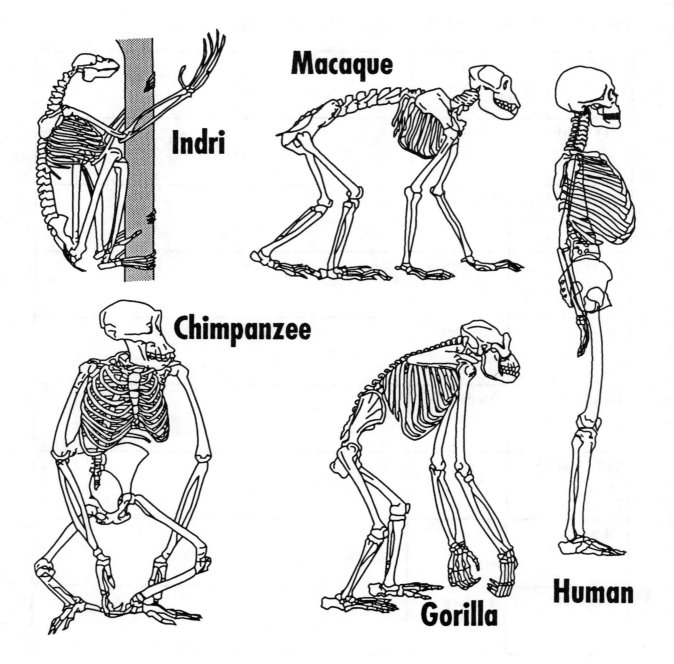

3. Draw a "family tree" of the primates, showing all the categories discussed in the Haviland textbook. (If you write the characteristics of the various primates near their names, this chart will be particularly helpful to study from.)

4. Knowledge of human skeletal anatomy is important for paleoanthropology. Here is a human skeleton for you to color.

Color the cranium *purple*. Notice how high and round it is, to accommodate our large brains.

Color the orbits *blue*. They face forward, allowing us to see stereoscopically.

Label the foremen magnum. Note its placement beneath the head.

Color the clavicle *orange* and the scapula *red*. The structure of the shoulder is related to our ancestry of brachiation.

Color the bones of the hands, which are prehensile and pentadactylous, *brown*. Now color the feet brown, too. See how they are adapted to bear the weight of a bipedal organism?

Color the pelvis *yellow*. It has been modified to accommodate bipedalism, too; it is thicker and wider than that of the other primates because it bears a great deal of weight.

Color the bones of the legs *green*. They are quite long and the structure of the knee allows full extension.

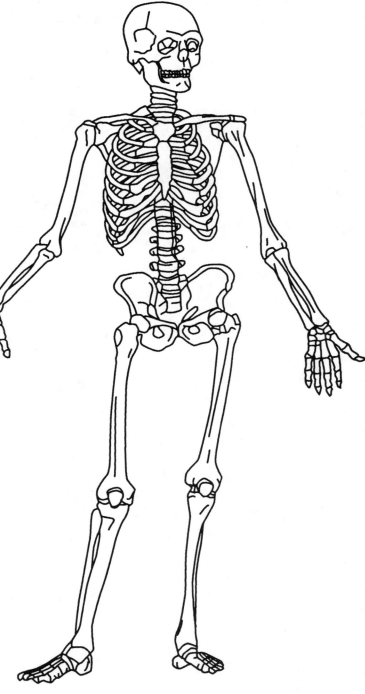

Multiple-Choice Practice Questions

1. Biologists today classify living things with the system devised in the 18th century by
   a. Charles Darwin.
   b. Carolus Linnaeus.
   c. Gregor Mendel.
   d. John Locke.
   e. Jane Goodall.

2. If two types of organisms have a similar body structure that is superficial rather than resulting from having a common ancestor (for example, both birds and butterflies have wings), we refer to these superficial similarities as
   a. analogies.
   a. homologies.
   a. sexual dimorphism.
   a. fovea centralist.
   a. scapula.

3. This type of animal has a constant body temperature, the limbs are beneath the body rather than beside it, it is relatively intelligent, and has mammary glands to feed the young after birth. Which of the following best describes it?
   a. reptile
   b. animal
   c. chordate
   d. dinosaur
   e. mammal

4. The primate suborder *Haplorhini* includes
   a. tarsiers.
   b. monkeys.
   c. apes.
   d. humans.
   e. All of the above.

5. The word "arboreal" means
   a. having the characteristics of arbs.
   b. living on the savanna.
   c. living in trees.
   d. preferring to live in caves.
   e. marine-dwelling.

6. Primates have a fovea centralist. What are the consequences of this?
   a. They can focus clearly on a particular object.
   b. They can hear sounds from two different directions.
   c. Their fingers are better at feeling.
   d. They are less likely to lose their teeth.
   e. Their brains have a larger emphasis on smell.

7. The area of the brain that has enlarged dramatically in primates is the
   a. cerebellum.
   b. cerebral hemispheres.
   c. medulla.
   d. notochord.
   e. smell brain.

8. The teeth of primates are
   a. more specialized in comparison with other mammals.
   b. all canines.
   c. less specialized in comparison with other mammals.
   d. larger in number than the primate ancestor from which they evolved.
   e. all premolars.

9. The primate skeleton reflects the importance in primate evolution of most of the following characteristics. Which of the following does it NOT reflect?
   a. a large brain
   b. upright posture
   c. increased significance of smell
   d. flexible limbs and hands
   e. The primate skeleton reflects all of the above.

10. The most helpless infant at birth would be the offspring of a
    a. femur.
    b. monkey.
    c. ape.
    d. human.
    e. gazelle.

11. On the basis of similarities and differences among living primates, physical anthropologists have constructed the following evolutionary chart: primitive primates probably resembled _____ , who then evolved into _____ , who evolved into _____, and eventually into _____.
    a. hominids/New World Monkeys/Old World Monkeys/apes
    b. New World Monkeys/baboons/apes/hominids
    c. strepsirhines/haplorhines/catarrhines/hominids
    d. chimpanzees/Old World Monkeys/New World Monkeys/hominoids
    e. orangutans/gorillas/chimpanzees/humans

12. Because modern strepsirhines have relatively large brains, flexible hands used in pairs, and mostly nails rather than claws on their digits, and because they also have pointed snouts, upper lips bound down to the gum, and moist, naked skin around their nostrils, they are said to occupy a place between insectivores and
    a. tarsiers.
    b. haplorhines.
    c. Old World Monkeys.
    d. New World Monkeys.
    e. hominids.

13. Tarsiers resemble monkeys in their noses and lips, and in that part of the brain that governs
    a. smell.
    b. hearing.
    c. touch.
    d. taste.
    e. vision.

14. You are visiting a zoo. There is a small, quadrupedal primate leaping around in its cage. It has a flat nose with widely separated, outward flaring nostrils and a prehensile tail. You classify it as a/an
    a. Old World Monkey.
    b. New World Monkey.
    c. strepsirhine.
    d. pongid.
    e. hominid.

15. The gorilla and chimpanzee both practice a distinctive form of locomotion called
    a. brachiation.
    b. knuckle-walking.
    c. bipedalism.
    d. quadrupedalism.
    e. slithering.

16. Position of a chimpanzee in a dominance hierarchy is affected by
    a. physical strength and size.
    b. rank of the chimpanzee's mother.
    c. motivation.
    d. intelligence.
    e. All of the above.

17. If you were to visit a primate group in the wild, the most frequent type of activity that you would be likely to see is
    a. sex.
    b. grooming.
    c. adults playing.
    d. infants being cared for by their mothers' friends.
    e. groups defending their territory.

18. The ability to make and use tools
    a. is present only in humans.
    b. is a significant part of the behavior of gorillas and orangutans.
    c. is present among chimpanzees but is rarely a significant part of the behavior of baboons and gorillas.
    d. is a significant part of the behavior of baboons.
    e. None of the above.

19. In the wild, _____ have not been observed making and using tools to the extent that chimpanzees do.
    a. ring-tailed monkeys
    b. orangutans
    c. bonobos
    d. rhesus monkeys
    e. gorillas

20. That these animals do have extraordinary capabilities is demonstrated by a captive _____who has figured out how to make tools of stone that are remarkably like the earliest such tools made by our ancestors.
    a. chimpanzee
    b. gorilla
    c. orangutan
    d. bonobo
    e. macaque

21. Which of the following primates has been observed hunting, killing, and eating small to medium-sized mammals?
    a. chimpanzees.
    b. gorillas.
    c. rhesus monkeys.
    d. bonobos.
    e. *a* and *d*.

22. Bonobos hunt, but in their case it is usually the females who do so, _____ being the most frequent prey.
    a. antelope
    b. zebra
    c. water buffalo
    d. monkeys
    e. giraffe

23. The apes are the closest relatives humans have. These include which of the following?
    a. gibbons.
    b. siamangs.
    c. orangutans.
    d. gorillas.
    e. All of the above.

24. Among bonobos, chimpanzees, and gorillas, both male and females are organized into _____.
    a. egalitarian groups.
    b. dominance hierarchies.
    c. balanced alliances.
    d. counterbalanced associations.
    e. blended coalitions.

25. Bonobos will defend their immediate space through which of the following?
    a. fighting.
    b. vocalizations.
    c. displays.
    d. facial contortions and spitting at intruders.
    e. *b* and *c*.

Answers to multiple-choice practice questions

1. b	8. c	14. b	20. d
2. a	9. c	15. b	21. e
3. e	10. d	16. e	22. a
4. e	11. c	17. b	23. e
5. c	12. b	18. c	24. b
6. a	13. e	19. c	25. e
7. b			

True/False Practice Questions

1. Several dozen species of primates are currently threatened with extinction.

2. Jane Goodall is best known for her long-term study of Indonesian orangutans.

3. Both fossil and biochemical data suggest that the orangutan is the most conservative (or primitive) of the great apes.

4. Orangutans and other higher primates are able to develop gestural language skills equivalent to those of a preschool human child.

5. Primates have retained less specialized teeth than other mammals.

6. Animals that habitually maintain a horizontal posture like dogs and horses have the foremen magnum facing downward from the bottom of the skull.

7. Catarrhine primates usually produce only a single offspring at a time.

Answers to true/false practice questions

1. T	3. T	5. T	7. T
2. F	4. T	6. F	

Practice Matching

1. Hominidae

2. Hylobatidae

3. Cercopithecoidea

4. Pongidae

5. Ceboidea

a. Family within Hominoidea consisting of Asian great apes

b. Family within Hominidae consisting of small apes

c. Superfamily of Old World monkeys

d. Family within Hominoidea consisting of humans, near-humans, and African apes

e. Superfamily of New World monkeys

Answers to practice matching

1. d   2. b   3. c   4. a   5. e

Practice Essay

Haviland uses primarily bonobos, chimpanzees, apes, and baboons to illustrate the various kinds of social organization found among higher primates. Compare and contrast the four, paying particular attention to what the behavior of these primates might tell us about the evolution of our own species.

Chapter 5
Fossil Primates

Synopsis

Chapter 5 traces the appearance and development of the earliest primates from the Paleocene to Miocene epochs. The adaptive radiation of the primates to various ecological niches is discussed and the major fossil finds reviewed. The chapter leads up to the threshold of the hominines.

What you should learn from this chapter

1. Understand the importance of studying early primates.
2. Understand the role of the environment in early primate evolution.
3. Know the basic sequence of early primate evolution and the characteristics of the representative fossils
   - Paleocene
   - Eocene
   - Oligocene
   - Miocene
4. Understand the importance of the ramamorphs as possible human ancestors.

Key Terms

adaptive radiation

ecological niche

Plesiadapiformes

Adapidae

Omomyidae

Parapithecidae

Propliopithecidae

quadrupedal

hominoid

ramamorphs

Hominid

dentition

Key Periods and Epochs

Match the period or epoch to its dates.

Triassic	230–180 million years ago
Eocene	55–34 million years ago
Paleocene	65–55 million years ago
Permian	280–230 million years ago
Oligocene	34–23 million years ago
Miocene	23–5 million years ago

Review Questions

1. Why do anthropologists study prehistoric primates?

2. What are the most common primate fossils found?

3. How does dentition assist in the identification and classification of fossil forms?

4. Describe a mammal-like reptile from the Permian period.

5. When did '"true" mammals first appear?

6. Describe a mammalian creature from the Triassic period.

7. What role did body temperature play in the evolution of the mammals?

8. What two factors inhibited the flourishing of the mammals prior to the Paleocene?

9. What environmental conditions allowed for mammalian adaptive radiation?

10. In what type environment (ecological niche) did our ancestors first appear?

11. What physical attributes were required for an arboreal existence?

12. What suborder of primate lived during the Paleocene? Describe the relevant finds.

13. What two primate families are known to have lived during the Eocene?

14. Distinguish between *Adapidae* and *Omomyidae.*

15. What environmental event marked the transition from Paleocene to Eocene?

16. What environmental event marked the transition from Eocene to Oligocene?

17. Why are Oligocene primate fossils rare finds?

18. What two primate families have been established from Oligocene fossils?

19. What is the significance of the new *Catopithecus* find at the Fayum desert?

20. What are the major theories regarding the origins of the anthropoids?

21. Describe *Aegyptopithecus* and identify its significance.

22. Describe *Proconsul* and identify its significance.

23. Distinguish between hominoid and hominine.

24. Distinguish between the two major groups into which late Miocene hominoids are divided.

25. What does the dentition of the ramamorphs indicate?

26. What is the importance of research in the savanna environment?

27. What are some advantages of a bipedal stance?

Fill-in-the-Blank

1. The first undoubted mammals appear during the _____ period.

2. Smell and hearing became highly developed in the mammals because many of them were _____ in their habits.

3. The real adaptive radiation and expansion of the mammals occurred after _____ million years ago.

4. The Paleocene creatures known as Plesiadapiformes probably ate mostly _____.

5. Eocene primates are divided into two forms, one resembling modern _____ and the other resembling modern _____.

6. _____ is now considered the oldest undisputed anthropoid.

7. The Fayum desert was in Oligocene times _____.

8. *Aegyptopithecus* means "_____."

9. The Catarrhine primates were restricted to Africa until _____ million years ago.

10. The Ramamorphs are also sometimes called _____.

11. Humans, orangutans and Ramamorphs all have _____ tooth enamel.

12. Early bipedal hominines probably carried both food and _____ in their arms.

Exercises

1. The maps below show the general course of continental drift over the past 200 million years. Color these maps, using different shades for each of the continental plates. What impact did continental drift have on primate evolution?

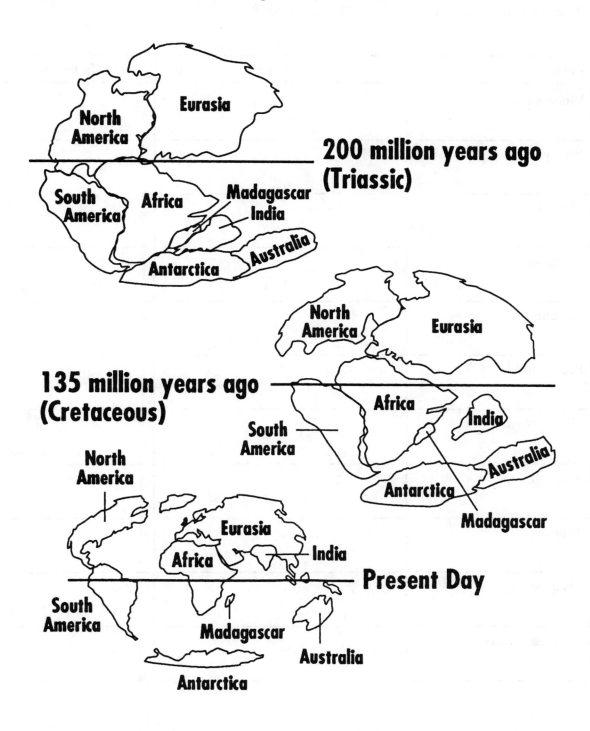

2. Here is a chart illustrating the major periods and epochs of biological evolution. At the right side of the chart, write in at which points the following forms of life appeared:

a) first reptiles   d) first primates
b) mammal-like reptiles   e) first hominines
c) first true mammals   f) genus *Homo*

Periods	Epochs	Life forms
Pleistocene		
Pliocene		
Miocene		
Oliocene		
Eocene		
Paleocene		
Cretaceous		
Jurassic		
Triassic		
Permian		
Carboniferous		

Multiple-Choice Practice Questions

1. The study of early primate fossils
   a. is easy because primates lived in conditions that promoted their fossilization.
   b. is difficult because primates lived in conditions that did not promote fossilization.
   c. is based primarily on dentition.
   d. depends a lot on our ability to infer the way a whole body functioned based on analysis of only part of its structure.
   e. All of the above except *a*.

2. Mammals evolved from reptiles _____ years ago.
   a. about 65 million
   b. by at least 180 million
   c. before 300 million
   d. about 4.5 billion
   e. about 10,000

3. Which of the following factors contributed to the success of mammals at the end of the Cretaceous period?
   a. Early mammals emphasized vision, whereas reptiles emphasized hearing and smell.
   b. The evolution of flowering plants provided high-quality nutrition.
   c. Mammals had variable body temperature and thus were more flexible than reptiles who had a constant body temperature.
   d. Mammals underwent a mass extinction at this time.
   e. All of the above.

4. Which of the following best describes the environment in which early primates emerged?
   a. Flowering plants had evolved, providing high-quality nutrition in the form of fruits, nuts, and seeds.
   b. An early primate could make its way from what is now North Dakota to what is now France because Europe was still joined to North America.
   c. A mild, wet climate supported the growth of an extensive belt of tropical and subtropical forests.
   d. All of the above.
   e. None of the above.

5. Which of the following statements about the Eocene epoch is CORRECT?
   a. Primates lived in North, America, Europe, and Asia.
   b. Few primates lived in Africa.
   c. All primates disappeared from North America by the end of this epoch.
   d. The Adapidae and Omomyidae initially spread widely and then almost disappeared.
   e. All of the above.

6. Which of the following statements expresses the significance that *Aegyptopithecus* has for our understanding of primate evolution?
   a. It is probably the earliest known Old World Monkey found in the Miocene epoch.
   b. It is probably the earliest known ape found in the Miocene epoch.
   c. Its lower molars have five cusps, indicating that it may have been ancestral to the Miocene hominoids that gave rise to humans and African apes.
   d. It was about the size of a squirrel monkey.
   e. None of the above.

7. The fossil primate Proconsul is interpreted as
   a. the earliest known Old World Monkey.
   b. a late-Miocene ancestor of African apes and humans.
   c. a descendant of the Ramamorphs.
   d. closely related to tarsiers.
   e. None of the above.

8. Which of the following statements about the ramamorphs is INCORRECT?
   a. Based only on the analysis of the teeth and jaws, researchers concluded that the ramamorphs might be ancestral to humans.
   b. Based only on the analysis of the teeth and jaws, researchers concluded that the ramamorphs must be ancestral to orangutans alone.
   c. Based on additional evidence that included skulls and limb bones, researchers concluded that the ramamorphs might be ancestral to orangutans alone.
   d. Researchers now suspect that ramamorphs might be ancestral to orangutans as well as to humans.
   e. All of the above are incorrect.

9. The *Catapithecus* finds at El Fayum are estimated to be about
   a. 55 million years old.
   b. 43 million years old.
   c. 37 million years old.
   d. 23 million years old.
   e. Unfortunately, scientists have no idea of how old the finds are.

10. Based on the characteristics of the teeth, ramamorphs probably lived
    a. at the edge of forests exploiting the high-nutritional foods of the savanna.
    b. in the deserts.
    c. in the top canopy of tropical forests.
    d. along river valleys.
    e. in mountains above the tree line.

11. Which of the following may have contributed to the development of bipedalism among the ramamorphs?
    a. the ability to increase the food supply by getting more seeds, leaves, and pods from spiny thorn bushes
    b. improved ability to carry offspring
    c. improvement in the ability to carry food from the open savanna to the safety of the trees
    d. increased ability to spot predators on the savanna
    e. All of the above

12. Carnegie Museum of Natural History's K. Christopher Beard's candidate for the earliest anthropoid is a controversial Chinese primate, about 45 million years old. He named the fossil _____, or "dawn ape."
    a. Lucy
    b. *Homo habilis*
    c. Kenewick Man
    d. Eosimias
    e. Piltdown Man

13. Although Beard and Ross MacPhee believe that the anthropoid lineage extends back at least _____ years, they also conclude that anthropoids are more closely related to omomyids than to adapids.
    a. 45 million
    b. 3 million
    c. 20 million
    d. 10 million
    e. 50 million

14. The ancestors of _____ and catarrhines shifted to a more herbivorous diet, with greater emphasis on arboreal quadrupedalism.
    a. tarsiers
    b. platyrrhines
    c. rhinicitis
    d. omomyids
    e. None of the above

15. The limb bones of the *Moropithecus* have recently been found at Moroto, in _____.
    a. Rwanda.
    b. the Congo.
    c. Burundi.
    d. Uganda.
    e. Zaire.

16. Sometimes called "sivapithecines" and sometimes "ramapithecines," this group was a various genera of hominoids lumped together as _____.
    a. Dryomorphs.
    b. Ramamorphs.
    c. *Proconsul.*
    d. *Morotopithecus.*
    e. *Ardipithecus ramidus.*

17. Many anthropologists have concluded that ramamorphs could have nothing to do with human origins. Rather, _____ were seen as the sole modern survivors of the ancient group.
    a. chimpanzees
    b. gorillas
    c. bonobos
    d. gibbons
    e. orangutans

18. Existing evidence allows the hypothesis that apes and humans separated from a common evolutionary line sometime during the late _____.
    a. Oligocene.
    b. Miocene.
    c. Paleocene.
    d. Eocene.
    e. Jurassic.

Answers to multiple-choice practice questions

1. e	6. c	11. e	15. d
2. b	7. e	12. d	16. b
3. b	8. d	13. a	17. e
4. d	9. c	14. b	18. b
5. e	10. a		

True/False Practice Questions

1. The adaptive radiation of the mammals did not really begin until after the mammals were present for more than 100 million years.

2. The earliest primates were probably insectivores.

3. The locality of El Fayum in Egypt is a key source of Eocene fossils.

4. It is now agreed that while the ramamorphs were ancestral to orangutans, the dryomorphs were ancestral to chimps, gorillas, and humans.

5. Bipedal stance may have made a contribution to bodily heat loss among savanna-dwelling hominids.

Answers to true/false practice questions

1. T   2. T   3. F   4. F   5. T

Practice Essay

Compare initial interpretations of the ramamorphs based on teeth and jaws with later interpretations based on skull and limb fragments. What is the current status of the ramamorphs in human evolutionary history?

Chapter 6
The Earliest Hominines

Synopsis

Chapter 6 covers the appearance of the genus *Australopithecus*. Environmental adaptation, subsistence, and the beginnings of culture of these earliest hominines are explored. The newly discovered transitional form, *Ardipithecus ramidus,* is discussed. Various theories of bipedalism are reviewed.

What you should learn from this chapter

1. Know the earliest hominine and its position in human evolution.
2. Understand the similarities/differences among the five species of the genus *Australopithecus:*
   - *A. anamensis*
   - *A. afarensis*
   - *A. africanus*
   - *A. boisei*
   - *A. robustus*
3. Understand how the change from thick forests to open savannas affected *Australopithecus.*
4. Recognize the main implications of bipedal locomotion.

Key Terms and Names

Ardipithecus ramidus

Genus *Homo*

law of competitive exclusion

Louis Leakey

Mary Leakey

Key Sites

Match the sites with the fossils found. Note: some relate to more than one fossil hominine!

Olduvai region   A. *afarensis*

Laetoli   A. *africanus*

Lake Turkana   A. *robustus*

Ethiopia   A. *boisei*

Transvaal   A. *anamensis*

Review Questions

1. What find in 1994 appears to be the earliest undoubted hominine?

2. When, where, how and by whom was the first australopithecine discovered?

3. What evidence indicates that the australopithecines walked upright?

4. What five species comprise the genus *Australopithecus?*

5. Why was "Lucy" considered such a significant discovery?

6. Describe the differences and similarities between *A. afarensis* and *A. africanus.*

7. What was the dentition of the australopithecines like?

8. How is intelligence inferred? What was the cognitive capacity of the australopithecines?

9. Describe the general features of *A. robustus* and *A. boisei.*

10. How do the recent finds of *Ardipithecus ramidus* and *A. anamensis* fit into the evolutionary picture?

11. Why does Haviland suggest that the australopithecines were probably tool users if not tool makers?

12. What is unique about Olduvai Gorge?

13. What physical changes did the opening of the savannas and the reduction of forest lands cause in early hominines?

14. What gender differences in food-getting strategies may have existed in australopithecine times?

15. What are some of the disadvantages of bipedalism?

16. Why is it unlikely that bipedalism evolved to allow males to acquire food for females?

17. Why is it unlikely that bipedalism evolved for non-territorial scavenging of meat?

18. What evidence has Pete Wheeler compiled to support the idea that bipedalism was primarily a result of heat stress?

Fill-in-the-Blank

1. *Ardipithecus ramidus* was discovered in _____ in Ethiopia.

2. The first australopithecine was found by _____ in South Africa.

3. *A. afarensis* and *A. africanus* can be described as looking like _____ from the waist up, and like _____ from the waist down.

4. Mary Leakey originally called *A. boisei* _____.

5. *A. robustus* and *A. boisei* had large teeth and heavy jaws, indicated that their diet was _____.

6. *A. anamensis* is believed to date to _____.

7. The australopithecines probably evolved from the ramamorphs via _____.

8. The first tools used by the australopithecines were probably _____.

9. A recent suggestion by Pete Wheeler relates the bipedal stance of the early hominines to _____.

Exercises

1. On this page you can see a comparison of chimpanzee, *Australopithecus,* and modern human.

   Color the *crania* and notice the differences in cranial capacity (brain size) among the three.

   Notice the *decreasing prognathism (jutting* forward of the mouth and jaw area) and the relative flatness of the modern human face.

   Label *the foramen magnum* on each skull, and notice the shift in its position. What does this shift indicate?

   Color in the *canines* and note what happened to them. Why?

   Look at the changes in the *dental arcade* from U-shaped to parabolic.

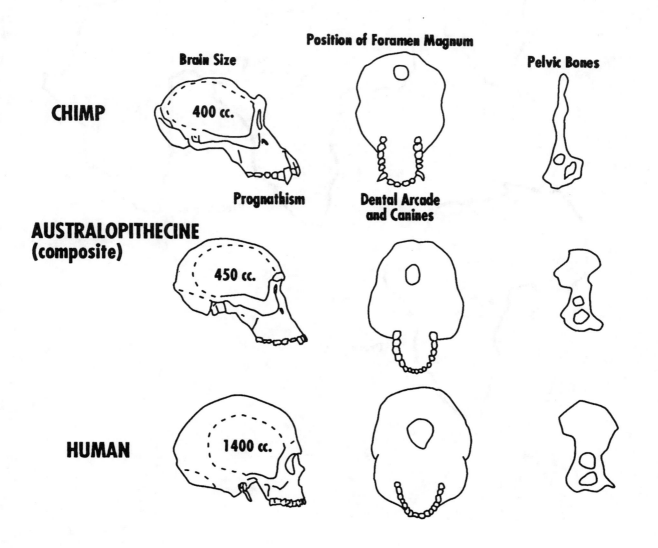

2. Here are maps of Africa showing the changing distribution of habitats from the late Miocene to the present. Color in the savanna, woodland, desert, rainforest and shrub areas on each. Then write two or three paragraphs explaining how these changes have impacted human evolution.

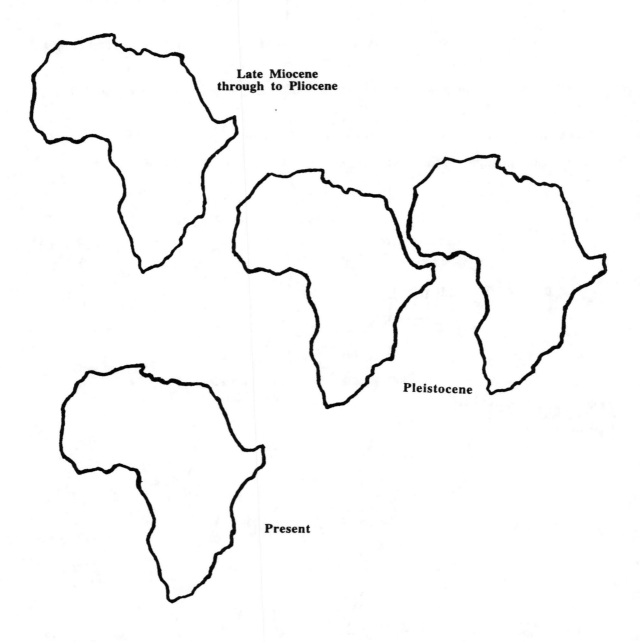

Late Miocene
through to Pliocene

Pleistocene

Present

3. On the map below, draw in the sites of the hominine finds covered in this chapter.

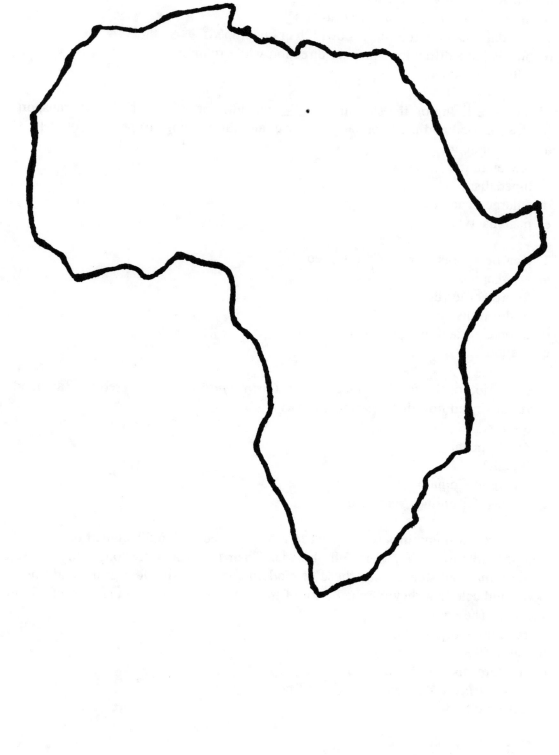

Multiple-Choice Practice Questions

1. A major disadvantage of bipedalism is
   a. greater visibility to predators.
   b. the soft underbelly is exposed to attack.
   c. bipedal creatures run more slowly than quadrupeds.
   d. bipeds have difficulty changing direction while running.
   e. All of the above.

2. If you were living on the savanna, ___.____ would improve your ability to transport food, spot food and predators at a distance, and throw things to protect yourself.
   a. pair-bonding
   b. scavenging
   c. bipedalism
   d. enlarged canines
   e. pentadactyly

3. The earliest tools were probably used
   a. as weapons.
   b. to protect territory.
   c. to dig roots.
   d. to butcher and prepare meat.
   e. *a* and *d*

4. The position of the foremen magnum on *Australopithecus* discovered by Raymond Dart convinced him that the creature was
   a. an ape.
   b. quadrupedal.
   c. bipedal.
   d. native to China.
   e. at least 65 million years old.

5. These ancient hominines were between 3.5 and 5 feet tall and weighed between 29 and 45 kilograms. They were fully bipedal. Their forearms were longer than those of modern man but shorter than those of modern apes. The shoulder girdle and finger bones indicate that they climbed a lot of trees. The brain varied in size from 350 to 485 ccs. They are
   a. the ramamorphs.
   b. early *Homo.*
   c. *A.* afarensis and *A. africanus.*
   d. *A. robustus* and *A. boisei.*
   e. early pongids.

6. The massive teeth, heavy jaw muscles, and sagittal crest of *A. robustus* and *A. boisei* indicate that they were
   a. omnivorous.
   b. vegetarian.
   c. primarily meat-eaters.
   d. tool users.
   e. tool makers.

7. The two most recent finds are
   a. *Ardipithecus ramidus* and *A. anamensis.*
   b. *A. afarensis* and *A. africanus.*
   c. *A. boisei* and *A. africanus.*
   d. *A. africanus* and *A. robustus.*
   e. *A. afarensis* and *Ardipithecus ramidus.*

8. *A. afarensis* fossils display a number of traits suggestive of a _____ ancestry.
   a. dryomorph-like
   b. ramamorph-like
   c. Plesiadapiformes
   d. Pesiadadapiformes
   e. *Proconsul*-like

9. By 2.5 million years ago, change resulted in the appearance of new forms including _____ and _____.
   a. *Ardipithecus ramidus* and *A. anamensis.*
   b. *A. afarensis* and *A. africanus.*
   c. *A. boisei* and *A. robustus.*
   d. *A. africanus* and *A. robustus.*
   e. *A. afarensis* and Ardipithecus *ramidus.*

10. For several years _____ has been studying just how stressful the savanna would have been for the first primates to venture out of the shade of the forest.
    a. Pete Wheeler
    b. Raymond Dart
    c. Don Johanson
    d. Louis Leakey
    e. Jennifer Thompson

11. Fossil flora and fauna found with _____ are typical of a closed, wooded habitat.
    a. *Homo habilis*
    b. *Ardipithecus*
    c. Neandertal
    d. *H. erectus*
    e. *Homo sapiens*

12. Besides making food transport possible, bipedalism could have facilitated the food quest in which of the following ways?
    a. With their hands free and body upright, the animals could reach otherwise unobtainable food on thorn trees too flimsy to climb.
    b. With both hands free they could gather food twice as fast.
    c. In times of scarcity, their ability to travel far without tiring would help get them between widely distributed sources of food.
    d. With the head positioned higher than in a quadrupedal stance, sources of food and water could be spotted from afar, thereby facilitating their location.
    e. All of the above.

13. Louis Leakey made it possible for _____ to begin her landmark field studies of chimpanzees.
    a. Dian Fossey
    b. Sigourney Weaver
    c. Jane Goodall
    d. Mary Leakey
    e. Jennifer Thompson

Answers to multiple-choice practice questions

1. a.	5. c	8. b	11. b
2. c	6. b	9. c	12. e
3. c	7. a	10. a	13. c
4. c			

True/False Practice Questions

1. Genus *Homo* contains three species.

2. The earliest and most primitive australopithecine was *A. africanus*.

3. Don Johanson is best known as the discoverer of *A. africanus*.

4. The intelligence of the australopithecines probably was about equivalent to that of modern great apes.

5. Early *Homo* coexisted with the late australopithecines for over a million years.

6. *Ardipithecus ramidus is* now thought to represent an intermediate form between the ramamorphs and the australopithecines.

7. The most widely accepted theory on the origins of bipedalism relates it to pair-bonding.

Answers to true/false practice questions

1. T	3. F	5. T	7. F
2. F	4. F	6. T	

Practice Essays

1. Explore the relationship between environment, diet, physical structure and behavior in the emergence of *Australopithecus.*

2. How is bipedalism inferred from the fossil record? What was the significance of the emergence of bipedalism for the hominines?

Chapter 7
Early *Homo* and Cultural Origins

Synopsis

In Chapter 7 Haviland considers the earliest representative of Genus *Homo*, *H. habilis*. Physical developments from the australopithecines to genus *Homo* are discussed and the appearance of stone tools is recognized as relating both to new subsistence strategies and to the evolution of intelligence.

What you should learn from this chapter

1. Know the difference between *Australopithecus* and *Homo habilis*.
2. Know the importance of the Olduvai Gorge and the Oldowan tool tradition.
3. Understand the implications of tool making for early *Homo*.
4. Understand the implications of meat eating for early *Homo*.

Key Terms and Names

Homo habilis

Lower Paleolithic

Oldowan tool tradition

percussion method

Adrienne Zihlman

Review Questions

1. Where was evidence for H. *habilis* first discovered? By whom?

2. Why is Olduvai Gorge so important in studying the Lower Paleolithic?

3. What form of heat exchanger was found in *H. habilis?*

4. How did Oldowan choppers affect food consumption?

5. What can gnaw and butcher marks on bones indicate?

6. What was the contribution of Adrienne Zihlman to our understanding of fossil?

7. What can comparison with contemporary and historically recent food foragers tell us about the life of *H. habilis*?

8. How might the early hominines have obtained scavenged meat?

9. What do we know about the relationship between gender and hunting among our hominine ancestors?

10. How did tool making affect the development of the hominine brain?

11. How can the study of modern primate behavior contribute to our understanding of cooperation and sharing among the early hominines?

12. Did *Homo habilis* use language?

13. How does the author of the Original Study relate the tree-climbing skills of early *Homo* to the scavenger scenario?

Fill-in-the-Blank

1. Louis and Mary Leakey found _____ at Olduvai along with *A. boisei.*

2. *Homo habilis* means "_____ ."

3. _____ probably gave rise to both early *Homo* and the *boisei-robustus* line of australopithecines.

4. The word Paleolithic means _____.

5. What is now Olduvai Gorge used to be _____.

6. Most of the places where Oldowan tools were found were _____ sites.

7. *H. habilis* was probably getting its meat from _____ rather than hunting per se.

8. One predator whose tree-stored kills may have been consumed by *H. habilis* was the _____.

9. In evolutionary terms, a population that puts its _____ at risk is less likely to jeopardize its reproductive success than is one that puts its _____ at risk.

10. _____ is an anthropologist who challenged the "man the hunter" view of human evolution.

Exercise

Complete this chart on the hominine fossils studied in Chapters 6 and 7.

Fossil Form	Where Found	When Lived	Characteristics
Ardipitizecus ramidus			
A. anamensis			
A. afarensis			
A. robustus			
A. boisei			
H. habilis			

Multiple-Choice Practice Questions

1. *Homo habilis* found by the Leakeys at Olduvai Gorge, with a cranial capacity of 650 to 690 ccs, and dated at about 1.8 million years ago; KNM ER 1470 found by Richard Leakey at Lake Turkana, with a cranial capacity of 775 ccs, and dated at about 1.9 million years—these are examples of
   a. gracile australopithecines.
   b. robust australopithecines.
   c. early *Homo.*
   d. *Homo erectus.*
   e. late ramamorphs.

2. The earliest known tool tradition
   a. is called Oldowan.
   b. begins about two and a half million years ago.
   c. marks the beginning of the Lower Paleolithic.
   d. All of the above
   e. None of the above

3. You are camping in Olduvai Gorge in East Africa. You find some stone tools. Part of the stone is untouched and feels like a rock worn smooth by wind and water action. One end has been hit—apparently by bashing it against a large rock, or by hitting it with another stone—and has a jagged cutting edge. The stone is a/an
   a. anvil.
   b. generalized chopping tool.
   c. hammerstone.
   d. percussion instrument.
   e. ancient flute.

4. Archaeological sites, dated at about two million years old, have been found that contain stone tools and the bones of many animal species. The bones have the marks both of stone tool cutting and carnivore damage. What interpretations have been made of these sites?
   a. They constitute home bases where early hominines brought their kill, butchered it, and shared it with each other.
   b. They constitute the dens of carnivores where prey was consumed.
   c. They constitute sites within a foraging area where hominids kept stone tools and where they brought scavenged or hunted food to cut up before they moved on quickly to avoid confrontations with carnivores attracted by the meat.
   d. All of the above have been proposed as possible interpretations.
   e. None of the above are considered viable interpretations.

5. Researchers have tried to establish "family trees" for the various hominine fossils between about four and one million years ago. The line represented by *A. anamensis* and *A. afarensis* has been interpreted by some people as ancestral to
   a. the robust australopithecines.
   b. *Homo.*
   c. the ramamorphs.
   d. *a* and *b*
   e. *a* and *c*

6. Hominine brains began to get larger
   a. about 2 million years ago.
   b. after bipedalism developed.
   c. as meat began to increase in the diet.
   d. All of the above.
   e. None of the above.

7. Paleoanthropologists _____ and _____ believe that the cut-marked upper limb bones of small, medium-sized, and large animals found at Oldavai Gorge demonstrate that hominines were butchering the meaty limbs with cutting tools.
   a. Jane Goodall and Dian Fossey
   b. Richard and Mary Leakey
   c. Henry Bunn and Ellen Kroll
   d. Louis S. B. Leakey and Mary Leakey
   e. K. Christopher Beard and Richard Kay

8. The early hominine Lucy was a _____.
   a. *Homo habilis.*
   b. *A. afarensis.*
   c. *A. robustus.*
   d. *A. africanus.*
   e. *A. anamensis.*

9. The antiquity of tree-caching behavior is difficult to prove, but it is supported by paleoanthropologist _____ excavations of ancient caves in southern Africa's Sterkfontein Valley.
   a. C.K. Brain's
   b. Adrienne Zihlman's
   c. Richard Leakey's
   d. Donald Johanson's
   e. Raymond Dart's

10. The work of _____ and her coworkers was crucial in forcing a reexamination of existing "man the hunter" scenarios, out of which came recognition of the importance of scavenging in early human evolution as well as the importance of female gathering and other activities.
    a. Dian Fossey
    b. Jane Goodall
    c. Adrienne Zihlman
    d. Mary Leakey
    e. Sheilagh Brooks

Answers to multiple-choice practice questions

1. c	3. b	5. d	7. c	9. a
2. d	4. d	6. d	8. b	10. c

True/False Practice Questions

1. *A. afarensis* was an ancestor of *H. habilis.*

2. *H. habilis* and *A. afarensis* coexisted at Olduvai Gorge.

3. The author of your textbook believes it likely that *H. habilis* used some sort of gestural language.

4. Increased consumption of meat began about 2.5 million years ago.

5. Among chimpanzees, meat is frequently shared.

6. *H. habilis* lived primarily in the Pliocene epoch.

7. Both the generalized chopping tool and the flakes created in its production were used by *H. habilis.*

Answers to true/false practice questions

1. F	3. T	5. T	7. T
2. F	4. T	6. F	

Practice Essay

Anthropologists use the presence of stone tools to argue that early *Homo* had "culture." How might we think about coming up with a definition of culture as a characteristically human form of adaptation?

Chapter 8
Homo erectus and the Emergence of Hunting and Gathering

Synopsis

Chapter 8 traces the spread of *H. erectus* out of Africa. The Acheulean tool tradition, use of fire, and other aspects of *H. erectus* culture are discussed. Physical features of *H. erectus* are contrasted with those of early *Homo* and modern *H. sapiens*.

What you should learn from this chapter

1. Understand where and when *Homo erectus* lived.
2. Be able to identify the major physical characteristics of *H. erectus*.
3. Comprehend the cultural development represented in the material record.
4. Know what the Acheulean tradition is and why it emerged.
5. Understand how the use of fire impacted the lives of our *erectus* ancestors.

Key Terms

Acheulean tradition

Paleolithic

baton method

Review Questions

1. When, where and by whom was *H. erectus* first discovered? What was it called?

2. In what regions have *H. erectus* remains been uncovered? What is the basic migration pattern as the hominines left Africa?

3. Compare *H. habilis* to *H. erectus.*

4. What is the story of the fossils from Zhoukoudian?

5. What four characteristics indicate that "Peking Man" was more modern than *H. erectus* from Java?

6. Compare *H. erectus* to modern humans.

7. Describe the skull of *H. erectus.*

8. What were the technological accomplishments of *H. erectus*?

9. Describe the Acheulean tool tradition.

10. What evidence exists to support the theory that the Oldowan tool tradition evolved into the Acheulean?

11. What are some examples of the diversification of tools during the Acheulean?

12. What were flake tools used for?

13. What does the diversity of tools indicate?

14. What Acheulean methods enabled the production of advanced axes?

15. What was the role of bamboo in *H. erectus* technology?

16. What evidence supports the idea that *H. erectus* knew how to use fire?

17. How might the idea of food cooking have emerged?

18. How might cooked food have affected the physical characteristics of the hominines?

19. What benefits were derived from the cooking of food?

20. What are some other ways the use of fire benefited *H. erectus?*

21. What evidence supports the idea that *H. erectus* hunted?

22. What evidence exists regarding the communicative capabilities of *H. erectus?*

23. What evidence points to an awakening of aesthetic sensibility in *H. erectus?*

Fill-in-the-Blank

1. Eugene Dubois called the remains he found in Java in 1891 _____.

2. Davidson Black discovered the site of Zhoukoudian after purchasing some _____ from a Chinese pharmacy.

3. The average cranial capacity of *H. erectus* is _____.

4. Acheulean tools are typically shaped like _____.

5. _____ are axes with a straight edge where the point would otherwise be.

6. The chopper-chopping tool tradition is geographically associated with the presence of the giant grass _____.

7. The _____ method of percussion manufacture involved using a bone or antler punch to hit the edge of the flint core.

8. Evidence from _____ in South Africa suggests that *H. erectus* may have used fire 1 to 1.3 million years ago.

9. The digestive tract of modern humans is _____ than that of apes, possible due to cooking of food.

10. _____ in France is a site where remains of *H. erectus* huts have been found.

Exercises

1. Shade in the geographic range of *H. erectus* on the map below. Mark the *erectus* sites mentioned in the textbook. How can we account for the spread of *H. erectus?* What were the effects of this expansion on further evolution?

2. Look at the skulls below, and use the terminology you have learned to describe the change observable from *Australopithecus* through *H. erectus* to *H. sapiens*.

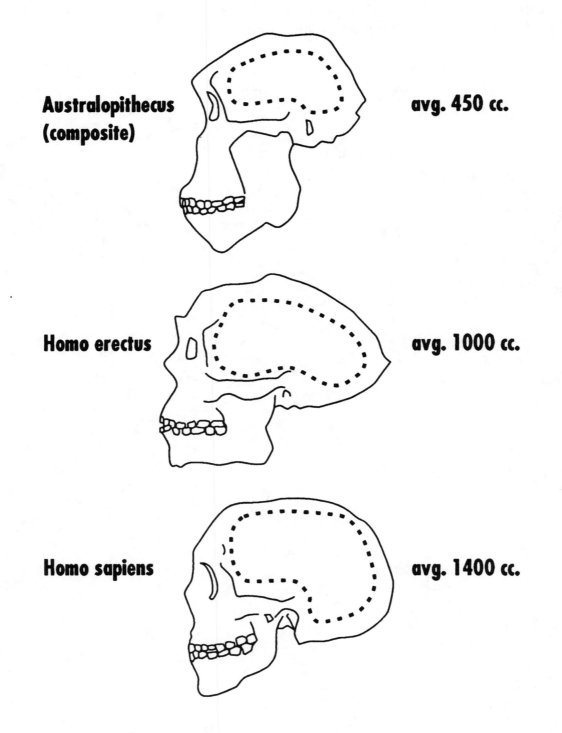

Australopithecus (composite)   avg. 450 cc.

Homo erectus   avg. 1000 cc.

Homo sapiens   avg. 1400 cc.

Multiple-Choice Practice Questions

1. Which of the following statements about *Homo erectus* is INCORRECT?
   a. Eugene Dubois named the fossils he found *Homo erectus*.
   b. What we call *H. erectus* today was first found in Java: a flat skullcap with enormous brow ridges and a brain size that looked smaller than the average size for *H. sapiens,* and a femur that indicated bipedalism.
   c. The first evidence for *H. erectus* indicated that the capacity for bipedalism was fully developed but the brain had not yet reached a size comparable to that of the average-sized modern brain.
   d. The first discoverer of *H. erectus* gave it a name that implied that it was part ape and part man, but that it walked erect.
   e. All of the above are correct.

2. According to information presented in the textbook, in which of the following places are *H. erectus* fossils NOT found?
   a. Java
   b. China
   c. Africa
   d. Europe
   e. the New World

3. The oldest and most complete *H. erectus* skeleton
   a. comes from Africa.
   b. comes from China.
   c. is about 1.6 million years old.
   d. *a* and *c*
   e. *b* and *c*

4. It is difficult to generalize about *H. erectus* in Europe because
   a. very few remains have been found in Europe.
   b. so many remains have been found that they haven't yet been organized.
   c. the remains are highly variable.
   d. *H. erectus* did not live in Europe.
   e. no one has studied *H. erectus* in Europe.

5. Based on characteristics of the adult skeletons, we think that *H. erectus* infants were relatively immature when they were born. Which aspect of the skeleton tells us this?
   a. size of hips
   b. size of brain
   c. length of legs
   d. length of arms
   e. size of big toe

6. The tool tradition of *H. erectus* called the ____ tradition.
   a. Oldowan
   b. percussion
   c. Acheulean
   d. baton
   e. Paleolithic

7. Which of the following statements about the Acheulean tool tradition is INCORRECT?
   a. In East Africa it apparently evolved from the Oldowan tool tradition.
   b. Acheulean traditions did not replace Oldowan traditions in East Asia for most of the Paleolithic.
   c. The characteristic tool of the Acheulean tradition is the hand ax.
   d. The Acheulean tool tradition includes cleavers and flake tools.
   e. The earliest Acheulean tools are found in Europe about 1.4 million years ago.

8. The Movius line refers to
   a. a type of fracture in an Acheulean tool.
   b. a geographical boundary that separates two Paleolithic cultures.
   c. the movement of *H. erectus* populations from Africa into Europe.
   d. a special bone on the cranium of *H. erectus*.
   e. a type of disease suffered by early *H. erectus* populations in bamboo forests.

9. The baton method
   a. was used by the australopithecines to kill lizards.
   b. was an early type of musical instrument used by *H. erectus*.
   c. was a tool-making method developed during late Acheulean times involving the use of bone or antler instead of a hammerstone.
   d. was a technique used by H. *erectus* to build a shelter of bamboo.
   e. was a method of catching bats in the cave of Zhoukoudian.

10. The systematic use of fire by *H. erectus* could have been used to
    a. clear trees through the jungles of Southeast Asia.
    b. improve the nutritional yield of many foods.
    c. thaw out frozen carcasses scavenged from the snow.
    d. chase predators from caves.
    e. All of the above.

11. An engraved ox rib that has no obvious practical function; the use of red ochre; evidence that a group of baboons were ambushed—all of these indicate that
    a. australopithecines were capable of symbolic thought.
    b. *H. erectus* might have been capable of symbolic thought.
    c. *H. erectus* could live in climates below 50 degrees F.
    d. *H. erectus* had clothing.
    e. *H. habilis* moved out of Africa into the cooler regions of Europe and China about 500,000 years ago.

12. It was on this continent that hominines, and later the genus *Homo*, originated.
    a. Australia
    b. Asia
    c. South America
    d. Europe
    e. Africa

13. Although some anthropologists have argued that the African fossils represent a separate species called _____ and would restrict *H. erectus* to Asia, neither detailed anatomical comparisons nor measurements support such a separation.
    a. *H. Ergaster*
    b. *A. robustus*
    c. *A. boisoi*
    d. *H. sapiens*
    e. *Proconsul*

14. Evidence from Indonesia demonstrates that *H. erectus* was capable of crossing open water by _____ years ago.
    a. 1.8 million
    b. 800,000
    c. 2 million
    d. 250,000
    e. 500,000

15. In which of the following ways does skeleton of *H. erectus* differ from that of modern humans?
    a. It is more heavily muscled.
    b. Its rib cage was conical.
    c. Its rib cage was barrel-shaped.
    d. Its hips were narrower.
    e. Only *a*, *b*, and *d*.

16. Although a mere 2% of body weight, the brain accounts for about 20% to 25% of energy consumed at resting metabolism in _____.
    a. *A. afarensis.*
    b. *H. erectus.*
    c. *A. robustus.*
    d. modern human adults.
    e *H. habilis.*

17. Evidence for hunting _____ years ago was discovered accidently in 1995 in the course of strip mining at Schoningen in northern Germany.
    a. 1 million
    b. 200,000
    c. 10,000
    d. 400,000
    e. 850,000

Answers to multiple-choice practice questions

1. a	6. c	10. e	14. b
2. e	7. e	11. b	15. e
3. d	8. b	12. e	16. d
4. a	9. c	13. a	17. d
5. a			

True/False Practice Questions

1. The first *H. erectus* find was made at the end of the 19th century.

2. The original Zhoukoudian bones were lost during the Japanese invasion of China.

3. Asymmetries in the *H. erectus* brain suggest right-handedness and possibly the capacity for language.

4. When viewed from behind, the *H. erectus* skull has its greatest width at the top and its narrowest at the base ("the trapezoidal cranium").

5. Acheulean tools have been found at Olduvai.

6. The Movius line was named after the Movius River, which bisects the Eurasian continent.

7. Kao Poh Nam rock shelter in Thailand, dated to 700,000 years ago, is known for evidence of cooperative hunting.

8. Fire in Europe and China may have been used to thaw animal carcasses.

9. Ambrona and Torralba are sites in Spain where the first evidence of fire has been discovered.

10. The *H. erectus* period was marked by an overall population increase.

Answers to true/false practice questions

1. T	3. T	5. T	7. F	9. F
2. T	4. F	6. F	8. T	10. T

Practice Essay

Describe the key sites at which remains of *H. erectus* and/or its culture have been found, assessing the significance of each for our understanding of human origins.

Chapter 9
Archaic *Homo sapiens* and the Middle Paleolithic

Synopsis

Chapter 9 covers the emergence of archaic *H. sapiens* and the transition to modern humans. The development of culture in the Neandertal period is described and theories about the relationships among various regions are compared.

What you should learn from this chapter

1. Understand where and approximately when archaic *H. sapiens* first emerged.
2. Know the cultural and physical changes evident in archaic *H. sapiens*.
3. Understand the issues surrounding the role of Neandertals in human evolution.
4. Understand the importance of cognitive capacity in the genus *Homo*.
5. Recognize the major lines of evidence for competing theories about modern human origins.

Key Terns and Names

Neandertal

Levalloisian technique

Middle Paleolithic

Mousterian tradition

Aurignacian tradition

Franz Weidenreich

Upper Paleolithic

the "Eve" hypothesis

mitochondrial DNA

Review Questions

1. Why might it be difficult to distinguish *H. sapiens* from *H. erectus* remains?

2. What advantages did the Levalloisian technique of tool manufacture offer?

3. What are some of the misconceptions people have of Neandertal's appearance?

4. What were the cultural capabilities of archaic *H. sapiens?*

5. What advantages did Mousterian tools offer over previous tool traditions?

6. What types of items were contained in a Mousterian "tool kit"?

7. How is it known that hunting was important to Mousterian peoples?

8. What evidence indicates that Mousterian peoples were more sedentary than previous people?

9. Describe the evidence for symbolic thought and behavior among Neandertals.

10. How does the author of the Original Study refute Binford's hypothesis of "opportunistic" hunting and scavenging?

11. What evidence supports the idea that Neandertal had a spoken language?

12. How might the human birth process have contributed to empathy as a species characteristic?

13. What two hypotheses purport to explain the transition from archaic to modern *H. sapiens?*

14. Where is there evidence of population replacement? Why might it have occurred?

15. Where is there evidence of multi-regional development? Why might it have occurred?

16. What evidence is cited to refute the coexistence of archaic *H. sapiens* and modern humans?

17. What is the "Eve" or "Out of Africa" theory? What evidence supports this theory?

18. In order for the "Eve" theory to be accurate, what chronological fact needs to be determined?

19. What criticisms have been levied against the "Eve" theory?

Fill-in-the-Blank

1. The _____ technique of tool manufacture entailed the detachment of flakes from a prepared core.

2. Neandertals lived from about _____ years ago to about _____ years ago.

3. In popular culture Neandertals are portrayed as classic "_____."

4. The large noses of the Neandertals were necessary _____.

5. The Neandertal skeleton was extremely _____.

6. _____ tools are characteristic of Neandertals.

7. People living in frigid climates need an abundance of _____ in their diets.

8. Binford believes that the kind of hunting premodern humans engaged in was primarily rather _____ than planned.

9. Human fetuses enter the birth canal facing _____.

10. At Shanidar Cave in Iraq it appears that _____ were placed at a Neandertal grave.

11. Aurignacian tools first appear about _____ years ago.

12. An alternative to the multiregional hypothesis is the "_____" hypothesis.

13. According to evidence from the study of mitochondrial DNA, modern humans share an ancestry in Africa _____ years ago.

Exercise

Locate the major sites covered in this chapter on the map below.

Multiple-Choice Practice Questions

1. Skulls from Bodo in Ethiopia, Swanscombe (England), and Steinheim (Germany) have been found, dating from between 300,000 and 200,000 years ago, that are considered to be
   a. primitive A. *africanus.*
   b. transitional between *H. habilis* and *H. erectus.*
   c. transitional between *H. erectus* and *H. sapiens.*
   d. primitive *H. erectus.*
   e. modern *H. habilis.*

2. The _____ technique of making tools involves the preparation of a striking platform at one end of the core, after which three or four long, triangular flakes are detached, leaving a nodule shaped like a tortoise shell.
   a. Oldowan
   b. Acheulean
   c. Paleoindian
   d. Levalloisian
   e. microlith

3. The name given to archaic *H. sapiens* in Europe and western Asia about 100,000 years ago is
   a. Ramapithecus.
   b. Neandertal.
   c. Cro-Magnon.
   d. Sivapithecus.
   e. Aegyptopithecus.

4. The midfacial projection typical of Neandertals of Europe and the Middle East is due to
   a. adaptation to a cold arctic climate.
   b. the largeness of the incisors and canines.
   c. large attachment areas for muscles that operate the thumb.
   d. robust muscles in the shoulder and arm.
   e. All of the above.

5. The archaic *H. sapiens* that lived in Africa, China, and Java at the same time as the Neandertals of Europe and the Middle East
   a. looked like the Neandertals.
   b. were more muscular and robust than the Neandertals.
   c. were a robust version of populations that developed later.
   d. had smaller brains than modern humans.
   e. were less robust than modern humans.

6. The typical tool-making tradition with which Neandertal is associated
   a. is called Oldowan.
   b. is called Achenlean.
   c. is called "Lower Paleolithic."
   d. is called Mousterian.
   e. is called Aurignacian.

7. Binford suggests that before the emergence of anatomically modern humans, meat was obtained primarily through
   a. cooperative hunting.
   b. stealing from successful hunters.
   c. scavenging and opportunistic hunting.
   d. horticulture.
   e. cannibalism.

8. Evidence about the cultural and social life of Mousterian peoples suggests that
   a. they were dumb brutes who had to move constantly to find food to eat.
   b. when someone died, they left them where they lay and moved on to another site.
   c. they wore no clothing and had no means of decoration.
   d. they did not have the capacity for rich symbolic thought.
   e. None of the above.

9. After the Aurignacian tradition spread into Europe by 35–40,000 years ago, the skeletons found with these tools are
   a. Neandertal.
   b. *H. erectus.*
   c. modern humans.
   d. pithecanthropine.
   e. australopithecine.

10. Mitochondrial DNA is located outside the cell nucleus and is not involved in sexual recombination of genetic material. Any changes that occur in this DNA are due to
    a. genetic drift.
    b. gene flow.
    c. convergent selection.
    d. divergent selection.
    e. mutation.

11. Most sites in Europe and Africa that date roughly between 400,000 and 200,000 years ago contain only parts of one or a very few individuals. The one exception is in northern Spain where the remains of at least 32 individuals of both sexes, juveniles as well as adults, were deliberately dumped by their contemporaries into a deep cave shaft known today as
   a. El Valle de las Lagrimas.
   b. Sima de los Huevos.
   c. Sima de los Esqueletos
   d. Sima de los Huesos.
   e. Cueva de los Huesos.

12. Around 200,000 years ago in Africa, a technological breakthrough called _____ the affixing of small stone bifaces and flakes in handles of wood to make improved spears and knives, took place.
   a. glueing
   b. smelting
   c. hafting
   d. wrapping
   e. grooving

13. _____ observes that such "classic" Neandertal features as sloping foreheads, bunlike appearance of the back of the skull and distinctively small mastoid processes that slope in are commonly present in medieval skulls from Denmark and Norway.
   a. Jennifer Thompson of the University of Nevada, Las Vegas
   b. C. Loring Brace of the University of Michigan
   c. Barry Hewlett of Washington State University
   d. Jose Cuellar of San Francisco State University
   e. Diego Vigil of University of California, Los Angeles

14. Which of the following qualities would describe Neandertal hunting practices?
   a. opportunistic
   b. deliberately planned
   c. unstructured
   d. logistically organized
   e. *b* and *d*

15. The hypoglossal canal in Neandertals is like that of modern humans and unlike that of apes. This feature indicates an ability to
    a. chew food thoroughly.
    b. communicate through a series of grunts.
    c. make the tongue movements necessary for articulate speech.
    d. carry a tune.
    e. digest food completely.

16. It is definitely premature to eliminate from the modern human ancestry all populations of archaic *sapiens* save those of Africa. Not even the case for exclusion of Neandertals is clear, but even if it were, this by itself would not be sufficient to rule out the _____ hypothesis.
    a. "Out of Africa"
    b. "Out of Asia"
    c. multiregional
    d. Garden of Eden
    e. None of the above.

17. As the number of human fossils has increased, and our knowledge of evolutionary processes has grown, _____'s ideas have been taken up by others and developed into the modern multiregional theory of human evolution.
    a. J. Relethford
    b. Louis B. Leakey
    c. Franz Weidenreich
    d. Charles Darwin
    e. M. Connor

Answers to multiple choice practice questions

1. c	6. d	10. e	14. e
2. d	7. c	11. d	15. c
3. b	8. e	12. c	16. c
4. b	9. c	13. b	17. c
5. c			

True/False Practice Questions

1. The first Neandertal find occurred just before the publication of Darwin's *Origin of Species*.

2. Early interpretations of Neandertal finds focused on the idea that they were deformed or abnormal.

3. Haviland believes that *Clan of the Cave Bear* gives a fairly accurate picture of Neandertals.

4. The average cranial capacity of Neandertals was the same or larger than that of modern humans.

5. Neandertal infants matured more slowly than our own.

6. Mousterian tool manufacture was more efficient than its predecessors because it got more inches of working edge per pound of flint.

7. Childbirth is more difficult for humans than for other primates.

8. At least some populations of Neandertals buried their dead.

9. The vocal tract of the Neandertals has been shown to be inadequate for articulate speech.

10. Franz Weidenreich believed in what later came to be called the "multiregional" theory of human evolution.

11. The "Eve" hypothesis suggests that humans share a common African ancestor who lived only 40,000 years ago.

12. Africans today have at least twice as much genetic variation as people from other continents.

Answers to true/false practice questions

1. T	4. T	7. T	10. T
2. T	5. F	8. T	11. F
3. F	6. T	9. F	12. T

Practice Matching

1. Le Moustier

2. Shanidar Cave

3. La Chapelle-aux-Saints

4. Klasies River

5. Qafzeh

a. site of a Neandertal burial

b. early Neandertal discovery of an arthritic old man

c. site which gave its name to the Neandertal tool tradition

d. "culturally precocious" archaic population in South Africa

e. site in Israel critical to discussion of multiregional versus single-origin hypotheses of human evolution

Practice Essays

1. Describe the culture of the Neandertals, showing how archaeologists make inferences from the material remains available to them.

2. Compare the multiregional theory of modern human origins with the "Eve" hypothesis, marshaling the current evidence for each.

3. Forensic archaeologists commonly work closely with forensic anthropologists. Describe their relationship.

Chapter 10
Homo sapiens and the Upper Paleolithic

Synopsis

In Chapter 10 Haviland describes the evolution of modern human anatomy and discusses the cultures of Upper Paleolithic peoples. The development of Mesolithic technologies is considered and two Mesolithic societies are compared.

What you should learn from this chapter

1. Know who the Cro-Magnons were and recognize their major physical features.
2. Understand the principles of Upper Paleolithic stone tool technology.
3. Appreciate the range and depth of artistic expression in the Upper Paleolithic period.
4. Understand the changes that took place between Paleolithic and Mesolithic cultural traditions.
5. Know the routes by which people migrated throughout the globe and the dates of the key migrations.

Key Terms

Cro-Magnon

blade technique

pressure-flaking

entopic phenomena

Paleoindians

cognitive capacity

Mesolithic

microlith

Natufian culture

Archaic cultures

Maritime archaic culture

Review Questions

1. Distinguish between the physical features of Cro-Magnon and those of modern humans.

2. Describe the Paleolithic blade. How was it made?

3. What are the advantages of pressure-flaking over percussion-flaking?

4. What advantages did the spear thrower offer Paleolithic peoples?

5. What physical/cultural phenomenon might have led to the development of improved hunting techniques?

6. What kinds of musical instruments did Upper Paleolithic peoples enjoy?

7. How might "Venus" figures have functioned?

8. What are some of the possible functions of Paleolithic cave art?

9. How did the scholar described in the Original Study attempt to experimentally explain the process of Upper Paleolithic cave painting?

10. Describe Paleoindian fluted points.

11. What environmental changes mark the transition from the Paleolithic to the Mesolithic?

12. How were microliths used?

13. What were the basic routes by which *H. sapiens* spread to Australia and the Americas?

14. Why does Haviland prefer the term "cognitive capacity" to the term "intelligence?"

15. What were the major features of the Natufian culture?

16. What were the major features of the Maritime archaic culture?

17. How might the evolving physique of *H. sapiens* have impacted gender roles in the Upper Paleolithic?

Fill-in-the-Blank

1. European remains from the Upper Paleolithic are often referred to as _____.

2. By about _____ years ago, Upper Paleolithic people "had the world to themselves."

3. The modernization of the face of Upper Paleolithic peoples was a result of the reduction in the size of _____.

4. The typical Upper Paleolithic tool was the _____.

5. The volcanic glass used by Upper Paleolithic people and adopted in the modern manufacture of surgical scalpels is called _____.

6. In pressure-flaking a piece of _____ is used to press flakes from a core.

7. Burins were mostly used for working _____.

8. Upper Paleolithic people were smaller than their predecessors because natural selection favored smaller body size as a form of _____.

9. The favorite game of European Upper Paleolithic people was _____.

10. There was a close connection between Upper Paleolithic art and _____.

11. The female figurines with exaggerated sexual and reproductive characteristics are called _____ figurines.

12. Lorblanchet recreated the conditions of Upper Paleolithic cave artists and learned to paint by the technique of _____.

13. Upper Paleolithic people migrated to Australia and New Guinea by _____ years ago.

14. The global lowering of sea levels created a land bridge between Siberia and _____.

15. The characteristic Mesolithic tool was the _____.

16. The geographic center of the Maritime archaic was the _____.

17. A key Natufian site was the village of _____.

Exercises

1. On the map below, show the major migration routes of *H. sapiens* into Australia and the Americas. List the dates near the routes you show.

2. Label the tools portrayed below and note when they occurred in the development of human culture. (These relate to Chapters 6 through 10.)

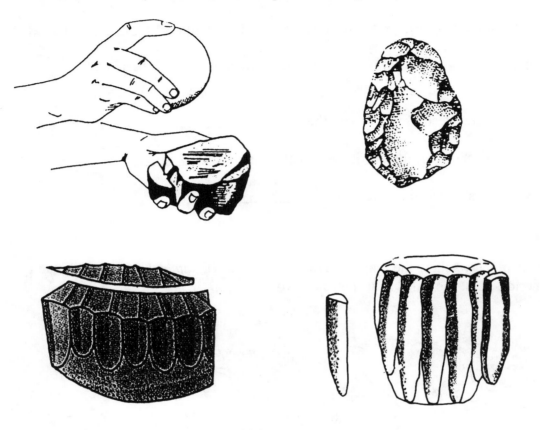

Multiple-Choice Practice Questions

1. Hominine fossils 30,000 years old are usually classified as
   a. Neandertal.
   b. Upper Paleolithic peoples.
   c. Cro-Magnon.
   d. anatomically modern *H. sapiens*.
   e. All of the above except *a*.

2. The typical Upper Paleolithic tool was the
   a. blade.
   b. baton.
   c. hammerstone.
   d. chopper.
   e. Levalloisian tortoise shell.

3. The Solutrean laurel leaf blades of the Upper Paleolithic
   a. were made with buries.
   b. were used to carve bone, horn, antler, and ivory.
   c. were used for the tips of arrows.
   d. were made from the pressure-flaking technique.
   e. gave rise to a more robust body.

4. Based on the fact that flutes and whistles made of bone have been found as early as 30,000 years ago, it is reasonable to assume that bows
   a. were used only for hunting.
   b. were used to make musical instruments.
   c. probably served as the oldest stringed instrument.
   d. were used to hunt Venuses.
   e. were used by female hunters.

5. The presence of sea shells and Baltic amber at sites hundreds of kilometers from the sources of these materials indicate that
   a. Neandertals were enslaved by Cro-Magnon populations.
   b. Upper Paleolithic peoples engaged in long-distance trade.
   c. Upper Paleolithic peoples possessed the wheel.
   d. use of fossil fuels was common by 35,000 years ago.
   e. the deserts were becoming covered with glaciers.

6. Paleoindians
   a. had distinctive fluted spear points.
   b. hunted large Pleistocene mammals and may have helped to drive them to extinction.
   c. lived about 12,000 years ago in Europe.
   d. *a, b,* and *c.*
   e. *a* and *b* only.

7. Cognitive capacity
   a. is a general capacity for appropriate behavior in a sociocultural environment.
   b. is based on a small number of genes.
   c. is found only among the Neandertals of Europe.
   d. has nothing to do with the evolution of the brain.
   e. has no survival value for humans.

8. The characteristic Mesolithic tool was a small, hard, sharp blade called a _____ that was used to make tools.
   a. Solutrean knife/other
   b. tortoise shelf Levalloisian
   c. Venus/Acheulean
   d. microlith/composite
   e. Neandertal/Middle Paleolithic

9. The Natufians
   a. lived at the eastern end of the Mediterranean.
   b. are an example of a Mesolithic culture in the Old World.
   c. lived in stone-walled houses in small villages, caves, and rock shelters.
   d. are the earliest known Mesolithic peoples to have cut grain and stored crops.
   e. All of the above.

10. The Cro-Magnons of Europe have suffered their share of idealization on the part of physical anthropologists; at one time they were depicted as having a somewhat _____ appearance.
    a. ape-like
    b. Christ-like
    c. god-like
    d. high fashion model-like
    e. grotesque

11. Modern faces and jaws are less massive than those of earlier peoples, however there are exceptions. For example, anthropologists _____ and _____ have pointed out that any definition of '"modernity" that excludes Neandertals also excludes substantial numbers of recent and native Australians, in spite of the fact that they are modern people.
    a. Wolpoff and Caspari
    b. Louis Leakey and Mary Leakey
    c. Richard Leakey and Mave Leakey
    d. Sheilagh Brooks and Richard Brooks
    e. J. Relethford and H. Harpending

12. In southern Africa regular use of yellow and red ocher goes back _____ years, with some evidence as old as _____ years.
    a. 10,000/20,000
    b. 300,000/500,000
    c. 50,000/100,000
    d. 130,000/200,000
    e. 1 million/2 million

13. Linguist _____, looking at the time it took various languages to spread from their homelands, estimates it would have taken at least 19,500 years for people to reach south central Chile.
    a. Gary Palmer.
    b. George Urioste.
    c. Johanna Nichols.
    d. John Swetnam.
    e. Noam Chomsky.

14. Although some kind of water craft had been developed early enough to get humans to the island Flores (and probably Italy and Spain) by 800,000 years ago, boats become prominent only in _____ sites.
    a. Lower Paleolithic
    b. Middle Paleolithic
    c. Upper Paleolithic
    d. Mesolithic
    e. Neolithic

15. When anthropologist _____ of Harvard University was to have some minor melanomas removed from his face, instead of allowing the surgeon to use a metal scalpel on him, he had a graduate student make a scalpel of obsidian by the same techniques used by Upper Paleolithic peoples, for the surgeon to operate with. After the procedure, the surgeon reported that the obsidian scalpel was superior to metal ones.
    a. John Shea
    b. Johanna Nichols
    c. Irven DeVore
    d. Richard Leakey
    e. J. Relethford

Answers to multiple-choice practice questions

1. e	4. c	7. a	10. c	13. c
2. a	5. b	8. d	11. a	14. d
3. d	6. e	9. e	12. d	15. c

True/False Practice Questions

1. Upper Paleolithic people lived longer than their archaic predecessors.

2. A blade is a flint tool at least twice as long as it is wide.

3. Obsidian, though useful to our Upper Paleolithic ancestors, is of little technological use today.

4. The bow and arrow made its first appearance in the Upper Paleolithic.

5. Musical instruments like whistles, flutes and stringed instruments made their appearance in the Upper Paleolithic.

6. The animals depicted in entopic art are the ones most often eaten.

7. Artists worked in Upper Paleolithic caves in near darkness, in the absence of any kind of lamps or other artificial lighting.

8. Ornamentation was common in the form of jewelry and beaded clothing in the Upper Paleolithic.

9. Some sort of watercraft must have been used by Upper Paleolithic people for their migration to Australia.

10. The Paleoindian peoples of North America hunted with spears tipped with specially fluted points.

11. The Mesolithic period began about 20,000 years ago.

12. The arrival of human populations in Alaska was the result of an actual migration of monumental proportions.

Answers to true/false practice questions

1. T	4. T	7. F	10. T
2. T	5. T	8. T	11. F
3. F	6. F	9. T	12. T

Practice Essays

1. Describe the florescence of the creative arts in the Upper Paleolithic period. What factors might have contributed to this "outburst of creativity"?

2. Discuss the diversity of Mesolithic cultures, comparing the Natufian culture of the Middle East with the Maritime Archaic of the Americas.

3. Changes in hunting weaponry and techniques had important consequences for human biology. What were those biological consequences?

Chapter 11
Cultivation and Domestication

Synopsis

In Chapter 11 the Neolithic revolution is defined and theories accounting for the emergence of food production are compared. Differences between Neolithic societies are described and the effects of sedentism on society are discussed. Finally, the impact of the agricultural lifestyle on human biology is considered.

What you should learn from this chapter

1. Know where and when plant and animal domestication first occurred.
2. Understand how and why people became more sedentary.
3. Know the difference between domesticated and wild plants and how this knowledge assists in our interpretation of past societies.
4. Understand the theories that attempt to explain subsistence changes in early humans.
5. Know the major consequences of food production.
6. Recognize some of the cultural indicators of a sedentary community.

Key Terms and Names

Neolithic period

domestication

unconscious selection

V. Gordon Childe

transhumance

vegeculture

horticulture

agriculture

pastoralists

Review Questions

1. What marks the transition from the Mesolithic to the Neolithic?

2. Compare the characteristics of domesticated plants and their wild counterparts.

3. Provide an example of unconscious selection.

4. What did the analysis of butchered sheep at Zawi Cherni Shanidar indicate?

5. What evidence exists indicating that food foragers controlled their environment?

6. What are some popular misconceptions regarding the change from food foraging to food production?

7. What is the "oasis" theory of the Neolithic transition?

8. What is the "hilly flanks" theory of the Neolithic transition?

9. What role might population have played in the Neolithic transition?

10. What environmental challenges did the Natufians face? How did they adapt?

11. How might the use of the sickle have influences the process of domestication?

12. What is the advantage of vegeculture?

13. How does food production affect the birth rate?

14. How does food production increase instability?

15. What evidence of domestication has been uncovered at Jericho?

16. What farming implements were used during the Neolithic?

17. Why did pottery making emerge during the Neolithic?

18. Describe Neolithic housing and clothing.

19. Describe the site of Jericho.

20. What evidence indicates the lack of a central authority and points to egalitarian social structure in Neolithic communities?

21. How is periodic physiological stress reflected in the fossil record of our Neolithic ancestors?

22. Why were Neolithic peoples more susceptible to disease than their predecessors? How did they survive?

23. The Neolithic period has been called a "revolution" in human culture. In what ways is the term "revolution" applicable? In what ways not applicable?

24. Why do anthropologists use the word "progress" with care in talking about the Neolithic transition?

Fill-in-the-Blank

1. "Neolithic" means _____.

2. The first and most intensively studied region to undergo the transition to food production was _____.

3. Wild cereals can be distinguished from domesticated ones by _____.

4. Wild pigs can be distinguished from domesticated pigs by _____.

5. V. Gordon Childe was famous for two of the most influential books ever written about prehistory, and _____.

6. Southeast Asians domesticated _____ before 5000 years ago.

7. About _____ per cent of the crops grown in the world today were domesticated by native peoples of the Americas.

8. Sanitary problems, close contact with animals, and density of human life in agricultural settlements all contributed to a rise in _____.

Exercise

Color in the major areas of plant and animal domestication on the map below, noting where possible which species were domesticated in each region.

Multiple-Choice Practice Questions

1. The Neolithic is different from the Paleolithic and the Mesolithic because
   a. it used microliths to make compound tools.
   b. it was distinguished by finely flaked tools.
   c. it was based on domestication of plants and animals.
   d. it depended on intensive gathering of wild plants and fishing.
   e. it was based on cooperative hunting of large herd animals.

2. A plant or animal that depends on another species for protection and reproductive success (in return for which it serves as food or a source of useful material) is
   a. domesticated.
   b. civilized.
   c. doomed to become extinct.
   d. always the product of conscious efforts by humans to plan food production.
   e. wild.

3. Which of the following would SUPPORT the idea that pigs had been domesticated at a particular site?
   a. smaller teeth than the teeth of wild pigs
   b. absence of horns in the females
   c. tough stems
   d. well-developed husks
   e. small-sized seeds

4. Which of the following statements about farming life as opposed to food foraging is CORRECT?
   a. Farmers have a more secure supply of food.
   b. Food foragers work harder to survive.
   c. Farmers eat choicer foods and a more varied diet.
   d. Food foragers are more likely to experience massive famine.
   e. None of the above.

5. Which of the following theories is at least somewhat supportable by the archaeological evidence?
   a. As glaciers retreated, Southwest Asia became drier, and people crowded into oases learned to cultivate plants and to capture and breed the animals attracted to the stubble of these plants.
   b. As glaciers retreated, Southwest Asia became wetter, creating more oases on which food foragers could rely for a more secure source of food.
   c. Food foragers compared the benefits of food production over the constant struggle to pursue wild food, and decided to domesticate plants and animals.
   d. As glaciers advanced and the climate grew colder, people were forced to develop food production to replace the dwindling supply of wild food.
   e. All of the above.

6. The shift from food foraging to domestication of plants and animals
   a. is always done consciously.
   b. can be done within a single growing season.
   c. always results in improvement of food supplies.
   d. often has long-term consequences that cannot be predicted.
   e. is the result of a few leaders making intelligent decisions.

7. Domestication of plants and animals was more likely to take place in
   a. open savanna.
   b. forests.
   c. temperate zones.
   d. environmentally diverse regions.
   e. oases.

8. In Southwest Asia, barley had tougher stems by 9,000 years ago, less husk by 8,000 years ago, and more seeds by 7,500 years ago. This means that
   a. barley was becoming domesticated.
   b. barley was degenerating.
   c. food foraging was more successful than farming.
   d. humans were colonizing the tundra.
   e. rice was being introduced from China.

9. Vegeculture is
   a. root crop farming.
   b. thought to be a more stable mode of cultivation than seed crop cultivation because many different species are grown in a single field.
   c. found in Southeast Asia.
   d. found in the Highlands of Peru.
   e. All of the above.

10. Which of the following statements helps to explain why food production spread to various regions of the world, displacing food foraging as a primary means of subsistence?
   a. By providing soft foods for babies, infants could be weaned earlier and women could become pregnant sooner; thus the birth rate for food producers was higher than the birth rate for food foragers.
   b. Farmers favor genetic uniformity in their plants; thus a disease that affects one plant is likely to affect all, and periodic famines can force people to move to new areas, carrying their food-producing technology with them.
   c. When times become difficult for food foragers, they may sometimes reluctantly borrow cultivation techniques from their neighbors as a last resort.
   d. All of the above.
   e. None of the above.

11. When continental uplift along the coast of Peru lowered the water table about 4,500 years ago, many marine habitats were destroyed. What did the population do?
   a. They began to grow plants cultivated by their highland neighbors a few thousand years earlier.
   b. They began to forage for new types of wild plant foods.
   c. They moved to new region where they learned to find new wild plants and animals.
   d. They migrated up the coast of Peru until they located still existing marine habitats like the ones they were familiar with.
   e. They died out.

12. Evidence of permanent buildings, ceremonial structures, tools for harvesting and grinding, and articles of trade would tell archaeologists that they were probably looking at a/an
    a. pastoralist society.
    b. food-foraging community.
    c. Neolithic community.
    d. industrial society.
    e. fishing village.

13. The presence of pottery at an archaeological site would be a good indicator that you were excavating a Neolithic community because
    a. fragile, heavy materials are more likely to be found in a nomadic food-foraging group than in a sedentary farming community.
    b. it indicates the ability to cook food, which was not done by Paleolithic peoples.
    c. it implies (but does not prove) that the community was sedentary and capable of supporting craft specialization.
    d. no food foragers ever make pottery.
    e. it implies that the sophisticated techniques required to make pottery were completely mastered.

14. You are an archaeologist excavating a site. You find a series of mud brick houses all roughly the same in size and decoration; there are no elaborate buildings set apart from the rest. The cemetery indicates that people were buried in roughly the same kinds of graves. From this you may infer that
    a. this was a small suburb of a larger city and was the place where members of a craft specialization lived.
    b. this was an egalitarian village lacking strong centralized authority.
    c. this was a highly stratified society.
    d. education was a very important means of moving up the social hierarchy.
    e. the society was governed by a king and a small group of advisors.

15. Widespread reliance on food foraging and relatively late development of the spindle and loom describe the Neolithic in
    a. Southwest Asia.
    b. Southeast Asia.
    c. Western Europe.
    d. the New World.
    e. Australia.

16. Which of the following statements about the effect of the Neolithic revolution on human biology is CORRECT?
    a. In contrast with Paleolithic peoples, Neolithic peoples were taller, more robust, and got better nutrition.
    b. Neolithic peoples show signs of chronic stress as indicated by high frequency of hypoplasias, effects of iron-deficiency anemia, and infectious disease.
    c. Mesolithic peoples were more likely to be affected by diseases arising from sanitation problems than were Neolithic peoples.
    d. Neolithic peoples show a greater number of injuries from compound microlithic tools.
    e. Neolithic peoples show signs of periodic stress, but their diet was adequate most of the time.

17. Which of the following statements SUPPORT the idea that the Neolithic was a progressive step up from the Paleolithic and the Mesolithic?
    a. Domestication of plants and animals could support more people.
    b. Food production allowed for the development of specialized crafts.
    c. A sedentary life and close association with animals exposed humankind to a new set of diseases and problems of hygiene.
    d. Food production led to diversification of cultures.
    e. *a* and *b* only.

18. There are numerous species that rely on some type of animal for which of the following?
    a. livelihood
    b. protection
    c. maintenance
    d. dispersal of their seeds
    e. only *b* and *d*

19. In China, domestication of _____ was underway along the middle Yangtze River, by about 11,000 years ago.
    a. maize
    b. legumes
    c. rice
    d. potatoes
    e. grain

20. What was distinctive in Southeast Asia was the domestication of root crops, most notably _____ and _____.
    a. potatoes and carrots.
    b. yams and potatoes.
    c. beets and potatoes.
    d. yams and taro.
    e. lettuce and tomatoes.

21. In the Americas, the earliest occurrence of maize is from deposits in _____ dated 7700 years ago.
    a. Mexico
    b. Peru
    c. Ecuador
    d. Panama
    e. Cuba

22. Increased dependence on farming is associated with _____.
    a. decreased fertility across human populations.
    b. an increase in the food supply.
    c. the stabilization of the food supply.
    d. the destabilization of animal populations.
    e. increased fertility across human populations.

Answers to multiple-choice practice questions

1. c	7. d	13. c	18. e
2. a	8. a	14. b	19. c
3. a	9. e	15. d	20. d
4. e	10. d	16. b	21. d
5. a	11. a	17. e	22. e
6. d	12. c		

True/False Practice Questions

1. When humans "domesticate" plants or animals they always do so intentionally.

2. Food production is a more secure subsistence strategy than food foraging.

3. The Natufians possessed sickles for harvesting grains and grinding stones for processing seeds.

4. Goats and sheep were probably domesticated by about 10,000 years ago.

5. Potatoes and maize were domesticated by native peoples of the Americas.

6. In humans prolonged nursing has a dampening effect on ovulation and hence leads to lower fertility.

7. People in Neolithic communities like Jericho probably remained in contact with food-foraging peoples.

8. The oldest known pottery is from Japan, dating to around 13,000 years ago.

9. A large proportion of the sedentary prehistoric population experienced chronic malnutrition and disease.

Answers to true/false practice questions

1. F	4. F	6. T	8. T
2. F	5. T	7. T	9. T
3. T			

Practice Essays

1. Anthropologist Jared Diamond called the development of agriculture "the worst mistake in the history of the human race." In what ways can the Neolithic revolution be seen as a negative occurrence?

2. Compare the various theories that attempt to explain the change in subsistence patterns from food collecting to food producing.

Chapter 12
The Rise of Cities and Civilization

Synopsis

Chapter 12 discusses the emergence of civilization as marked by the transition from Neolithic villages to urban life. The culture changes of this transition are discussed using examples from the major ancient civilizations. The textbook reviews the four more prominent theories that attempt to explain the emergence of civilization and offers some thoughts on the ramifications of this development.

What you should learn from this chapter

1. Know where and approximately when the first civilizations arose.
2. Understand the four culture changes that mark the transition from Neolithic village life to urban life:
   - agricultural innovation
   - diversification of labor
   - central government
   - social stratification
3. Know how archaeologists determine:
   - the existence of a central government
   - the existence of social classes
4. Understand the four theories that attempt to explain the rise of civilization:
   - hydraulic
   - trade
   - circumscription
   - religion
5. Know some of the ramifications of the development of civilization.

Key Terms

civilization

hydraulic theory

Bronze Age

Review Questions

1. What two characteristics are indicators of civilization or cities?

2. Why was an expanded study required at Tikal?

3. Why was an understanding of population size and density important in researching?

4. How can social organization be determined archaeologically?

5. How was the overall size of Tikal estimated?

6. What problems prevented excavating all structures around Tikal?

7. Why were test pits sunk at Tikal after other structures/features were thoroughly excavated?

8. What geographic evidence exists for Tikal's role in trade?

9. Give some examples of the "diversification of labor" at Tikal.

10. What major role might religion have played at Tikal?

11. What "agricultural innovation" supported an increase in population at Tikal?

12. What evidence do archaeologists have of the "critical point" reached at Tikal?

13. List the four cultural changes that mark the transition from Neolithic to urban life.

14. Give some examples of "agricultural innovation."

15. What three types of agricultural systems may be attributed to the Maya at Tikal?

16. What occurred at the city of Lagash to enable such a variety of skilled labor to exist?

17. What is the Bronze Age?

18. Why did the Aztecs and Maya not use metal tools?

19. Did boats play an important role in the development of early civilizations? Why?

20. Of what importance was astronomy to ancient civilization?

21. What are some of the archaeological indicators of a centralized government?

22. List at least four distinct functions of a centralized government.

23. What major benefits were derived from a centralized government?

24. How was writing first used in the Old World?

25. Distinguish between pictographs and ideograms.

26. What are four ways archaeologists determine social status?

27. What are some characteristics of Neolithic graves?

28. How can dwellings indicate social class? Burials?

29. What are the four main theories of civilization's emergence? Which three are ecological, and why?

30. What is the common thread linking all of the theories?

31. Briefly explain the hydraulic or irrigation theory.

32. What is the major criticism levied against the hydraulic theory?

33. How does trade enable the growth of civilization?

34. Explain social and environmental circumscription.

35. Describe the excavation of the Moche tomb recounted in the Original Study.

36. What are some of the problems that continue to plague civilization?

Exercise

Shade in and label the six early states on the map below. What can you notice about their general geographic alignment?

Multiple-Choice Practice Questions

1. "Civilization"
   a. comes from the Latin word for "well-behaved."
   b. can exist only with industrial technology.
   c. is not found in third-world countries.
   d. occurred first in preindustrial cities.
   e. None of the above.

2. Sumer, the world's first civilization,
   a. developed 5,000 years ago in the Indus Valley.
   b. developed 5,000 years ago in Mesoamerica.
   c. developed 5,000 years ago in Mesopotamia.
   d. developed 6,000 years ago in China.
   e. None of the above.

3. Which of the following statements about Tikal is INCORRECT?
   a. Tikal was a product of Maya civilization.
   b. Tikal was built in a rainforest region.
   c. At the city's height, it contained as many as 50,000 people.
   d. By A.D. 600, Tikal was composed of small, dispersed populations relying on slash-and-burn agriculture.
   e. Tikal may have exported flint.

4. Farming methods changed dramatically during the shift from Neolithic village life to urban life. Tikal adjusted to this change by
   a. reducing its population densities so that there were fewer mouths to feed.
   b. building elaborate irrigation systems, including dikes, canals, and reservoirs.
   c. switching from wild to cultivated rice.
   d. relying on the breadfruit tree.
   e. cultivating trees and constructing raised fields.

5. The city of Tikal was governed by
   a. an egalitarian council of women.
   b. a hereditary ruling dynasty.
   c. a council of elders based on kinship.
   d. elected senators.
   e. craft guilds.

6. High crop yields can encourage innovation because
    a. more protein is available so the brain functions more efficiently.
    b. more food supports more people, some of whom might be creative.
    c. more food allows some people to specialize and become experts in nonagricultural activities.
    d. more food frees people to become involved with trade for new items.
    e. None of the above

7. The Aztecs and Mayas did not have the same kind of Bronze Age as did the Old World because
    a. they were less innovative.
    b. they did not have access to the natural resources to make bronze.
    c. they did not require metal weapons as their enemies were weak.
    d. their environment supplied them with obsidian, which was adequate for their needs.
    e. civilization emerged earlier in the Old World.

8. Which of the following discoveries at an archaeological site are indicators of a strong centralized government?
    a. The settlement was laid out in a very definite pattern.
    b. Existence of a drainage system.
    c. A centrally located large building.
    d. Clay tablets with incisions.
    e. All of the above.

9. A picture that represents an idea rather than an object is called a/an
    a. pictograph.
    b. hieroglyph.
    c. ideogram.
    d. phoneme.
    e. icon.

10. Wedge-shaped marks (cuneiform) that stood for words and later for syllables developed about 6,000 years ago in
    a. China.
    b. Peru.
    c. Mesoamerica.
    d. the Indus Valley.
    e. Mesopotamia.

11. Hammurabi is considered remarkable because
    a. he emerged as king from an egalitarian society.
    b. he developed the ideogramatic system of writing.
    c. he developed a standardized and detailed legal code.
    d. he stripped away the wealth of the elite and made all citizens equally wealthy.
    e. None of the above.

12. In the sixteenth century, just prior to the arrival of the Spanish, the Inca Empire of
    _____ covered a vast area roughly 500 miles wide and 2,500 miles long. It
    included millions of people of diverse _____ groups.
    a. Mesoamerica/ economic
    b. Brazil/ economic
    c. Peru/ ethnic
    d. Chile/ ethnic
    e. Mexico/ religious

13. You have uncovered a burial at an excavation. To support your notion that the society
    you are investigating was a stratified one, you hope to find
    a. the body in the fetal position.
    b. little variety in grave goods.
    c. evidence of a poor diet.
    d. only utensils, figurines, and personal possessions.
    e. None of the above.

14. A key ingredient in all the theories that attempt to explain the emergence of
    civilization is
    a. social stratification.
    b. an egalitarian populous.
    c. a centralized government.
    d. diversification of labor.
    e. agricultural innovation.

15. The four theories of the emergence of civilization include all of the following
    EXCEPT
    a. hydraulic.
    b. religion.
    c. warfare.
    d. circumscription.
    e. trade.

16. Which of the following SUPPORTS Wittfogel's hydraulic theory of civilization?
    a. Cities were established in Mesopotamia by 2000 B.C, and irrigation was regulated by local temples on a small scale.
    b. Highland New Guinea had an egalitarian social structure and large-scale irrigation systems.
    c. Ancient Egyptian civilization had an elaborate priesthood and specialists in astronomy who built dikes and canals and tried to predict when the Nile would flood; these specialists formed the core of an elite social class having direct input to the governing body.
    d. All of the above.
    e. None of the above.

17. The Maya city of Tikal was situated between two rivers. With only this in mind, the theory of the emergence of civilization that explains Tikal's development is
    a. the hydraulic theory.
    a. the circumscription theory.
    a. the religion (beliefs) theory.
    a. the trade theory.
    a. None of the above.

18. According to Carneiro's theory of environmental and social circumscription, the situation most likely to give rise to civilization is
    a. when Neolithic villagers first began to expand into the vast interior of central Europe.
    b. when settlers moving along the Rhone and Rhine made it to the western coast of Europe and found themselves hemmed in by the sea while other settlements had been established behind them.
    c. when seafaring peoples began to populate the Pacific islands.
    d. None of the above.
    e. All of the above.

19. Which of the following problems are more likely to be found in civilization as opposed to a food-foraging band?
    a. disease resulting from the accumulation of waste
    b. diseases such as flu, mumps, smallpox, rubella . . .
    c. interclass problems arising from unequal access to resources
    d. None of the above
    e. All of the above

20. The inhabitants of _____, in southern Mesopotamia, developed the world's first civilization about 5,000 years ago.
    a. Bagdad
    b. Tehran
    c. Sumer
    d. Jericho
    e. Teotihuacan

21. The Americas' first great experience in urbanism is _____.
    a. Macchu Pichu.
    b. Tikal.
    c. Chichen Itza.
    d. Teotihuacan.
    e. Tulum

22. An indication that Teotihuacan had strong centralized control is evidenced by the _____.
    a. law codes.
    b. forced relocation of people from the Basin of Mexico.
    c. temple records.
    d. All of the above.
    e. None of the above.

23. This theory for the emergence of civilization recognizes the systemic nature of society and the impact of the environment in shaping social and cultural behavior, but recognizes that forceful leaders in any society strive to advance their material or political positions through self-serving actions.
    a. environmental and social circumscription theory
    b. trade networks theory
    c. hydraulic theory
    d. functional theory
    e. action theory

24. Early cities tended to be disease-ridden places, with relatively high death rates. At _____, for instance, very high infant and child mortality rates set a limit to the city's growth.
    a. Teotihuacan
    b. Tenochtitlan
    c. Tikal
    d. Chichen Itza
    e. San Pablo la Laguna

Answers to multiple-choice practice questions

1. d	7. d	13. e	19. e
2. c	8. e	14. c	20. c
3. d	9. c	15. c	21. d
4. e	10. e	16. c	22. d
5. b	11. c	17. d	23. e
6. c	12. c	18. b	24. a

True/False Practice Questions

1. The English word "civilization" stems from a Latin word relating to "city."

2. Tikal was one of the largest Aztec cities, reaching a size of over 100,000 inhabitants.

3. Slash-and-burn was the primary mode of subsistence in early Tikal.

4. The Bronze Age in Southwest Asia began in about 5,000 B.C.

5. Ancient Maya methods of agriculture could well be applied fruitfully today in tropical forested countries.

6. Some form of recorded information is a critical feature of civilization.

7. The Moche kingdom flourished on the north coast of Peru between A.D. 100 and 800.

8. Although the Moche were warlike, there is no evidence that they practice human sacrifice.

9. The anthropologist who came up with the theory of environmental and social circumscription was Robert Carneiro.

Answers to true/false practice questions

1. T	4. T	6. T	8. F
2. F	5. T	7. T	9. T
3. T			

Practice Essay

Trace how the Maya city of Tikal evolved. Be sure to include examples of cultural change and determine how *each* theory of the emergence of civilization might apply. Evaluate each theory as it applies to the emergence and development of Tikal.

Chapter 13
Modern Human Diversity

Synopsis

Chapter 13 examines the variations observable in human populations. The chapter explores the concept of "race" and suggests it is more productive to analyze specific traits rather than packages of traits. The continuing impact of evolution on human populations is considered.

What you should learn from this chapter

1. Know how anthropologists have classified *Homo sapiens*.
2. Understand the limitations of biological classification of humans.
3. Understand the role the environment plays in determining physical characteristics.
4. Understand the relationship between enculturation and biology in determining assumed behavioral differences in humans.

Key Terms and Names

polymorphic

faunal region

polytypic

race

epicanthic eye fold

melanin

racism

lactose

lactase

Review Questions

1. What advantage does a polymorphic species enjoy?

2. Provide an example of a polytypic species.

3. How did early scholars define races?

4. Why were these early classifications problematic?

5. What are three explanations for the function of geographically variable human traits, as presented in the Original Study?

6. What is meant by "genetically-open races"?

7. Provide some examples of physical adaptation based on climatic variability.

8. How does body build relate to climatic zone?

9. How does nose shape relate to climatic zone?

10. How does skin color relate to geography?

11. Why are intelligence tests probably an inaccurate measure of intelligence?

12. What evidence exists for the hereditary control of intelligence?

13. What evidence exists for environmental influence on intelligence?

14. What do intelligence tests really measure?

15. In what ways can culture act as an agent of biological selection?

16. Why is the emergence of new diseases of interest to anthropologists?

Fill-in-the-Blank

1. A geographic region with its own distinctive assemblage of animal life is called a
_____.

2. When a polymorphic species is divided into geographically dispersed populations, it
usually is _____: that is, genetic variability is unevenly expressed.

3. The chemical responsible for dark skin pigmentation is _____.

4. People native to regions where the climate is cold tend to have _____ body
build.

5. _____ caused by a deficiency of Vitamin D could interfere with a
woman's capacity to give birth.

6. A new book on IQ differences by Herrnstein and Murray called _____ has
provoked a storm of controversy.

Multiple-Choice Practice Questions

1. By the time *H. erectus* appears in the fossil record, populations were living in Africa,
   Southeast Asia, Europe, and China. They were able to adapt to these different
   environments because they were
   a. ethnic.
   b. racist.
   c. polytypic.
   d. polymorphic.
   e. faunal.

2. American Indians have a high frequency of the O allele in the A-B-O blood type
   system, whereas the B allele has its highest frequency in Asia. This is an example of
   humans being
   a. climatic.
   b. polymorphic.
   c. polytypic.
   d. influenced by culture.
   e. hereditarian.

3. When looking at the distribution of genes responsible for human skin color and blood type, we find that the genes resulting in darker skin color increase in frequency from northern Europe to Central Africa, and that the gene for blood type B
   a. also increases in frequency from northern Europe to Central Africa.
   b. is present in Europe but absent from Africa.
   c. increases in frequency from western Europe to eastern Europe.
   d. is linked with the gene for skin color.
   e. is linked with the gene for lactase.

4. How was the approach to racial classification proposed by Coon, Garn, and Birdsell different from previous systems of racial classification?
   a. They decided not to use the concept of race but to focus on individual traits.
   b. They said that races were populations whose similarities were due to adaptation to similar environmental conditions, and that when the environment changed the characteristics of the groups living there would also change.
   c. They said that there had been so much racial mixture that there were no more pure races any more.
   d. They said that all members of a particular race had to have a certain set of characteristics.
   e. None of the above.

5. The problem with using the concept of race to understand polytypic variation in humans IS
   a. the traits that are used to define a race are arbitrary; they could include shape of ear lobes, number of fingers, or skin color.
   b. the traits that are used to define a race do not always go together; the genes for dark skin color, for example, may exist in a person who has genes for straight hair and blue eyes.
   c. alleles usually exist in all populations; what varies is the frequency.
   d. All of the above.
   e. None of the above.

6. Which of the following statements about race is INCORRECT?
   a. The differences between individuals in a racial group may be greater than the differences between racial groups.
   b. Races are distinguished by their having genes that no other race has.
   c. Gene flow between populations occurred only after the development of farming.
   d. Differences between individuals in a racial group are always smaller than the differences between racial groups.
   e. All of the above except a.

7. How do many anthropologists talk about human variation in such a way that they avoid the problems associated with the concept of race?
   a. They pay attention only to cultural categories and avoid biological traits.
   b. They accept the idea that it is impossible to study pure races today, and that they must reconstruct them from an analysis of racial mixtures.
   c. They concentrate on explaining why the frequency of particular alleles is higher or lower in certain populations, and avoid using the term race.
   d. They choose what they consider to be the single most important trait in defining a racial group.
   e. They do not talk about human variation at all.

8. A person with larger body bulk and shorter extremities would
   a. get rid of excess heat quickly in hot climates.
   b. conserve body heat in cold climates.
   c. die in temperate climates.
   d. overheat and die in cold climates.
   e. be less likely to wear clothing than a long, slender person.

9. Features of the body that are adaptive in cold climates include
   a. longer, larger noses.
   b. epicanthic eye fold.
   c. round head.
   d. fatty deposits on face.
   e. All of the above.

10. Skin color is the result of
    a. the foods that you eat.
    b. the transparency or thickness of the skin.
    c. reflected color from blood vessels.
    d. the pigments carotene and melanin.
    e. All of the above except *a*.

11. A doctrine by which one group asserts its biological superiority over another is
    a. race.
    b. racism.
    c. polytypic.
    d. polymorphic.
    e. epicanthic.

12. The fact that children in rural areas average about 15 points lower on IQ scores than urban children, and that children born later in large families have lower IQ scores than first-born children indicates that
    a. the major cause of intelligence is heredity.
    b. environment has very little influence on intelligence.
    c. some races are more intelligent than others.
    d. environment has an enormous effect on intelligence.
    e. one's race is determined by birth order and where one lives.

13. For a biologist to say that a trait such as intelligence is "heritable" means that
    a. it is inevitable that you will have the intelligence that is coded in your genes.
    b. your intelligence depends on the interaction between your genes and the environment.
    c. your intelligence depends solely on the environment in which you were raised.
    d. All of the above.
    e. None of the above.

14. The "hereditarian fallacy" as explained by Gould is
    a. the fallacy that intelligence, as measured by IQ tests, is affected by heredity.
    b. is the fallacious assumption that if a trait is affected by heredity, you must have it.
    c. is the fallacious assumption that if differences within a group are due to the influence of heredity, then you can estimate the contribution that heredity makes to differences between groups.
    d. *a, b*, and *c*.
    e. *b* and *c* only.

15. Which of the following statements about intelligence is CORRECT?
    a. Intelligence is what is measured by IQ tests.
    b. IQ tests measure a single ability, comparable to the use of a blood test to measure blood type.
    c. Intelligence is a product of genes and is influenced very little by the environment.
    d. All of the above.
    e. None of the above.

16. The frequency of the gene responsible for porphyria is likely to decrease in the population under which of the following conditions?
    a. in rural conditions with little medical technology
    b. in cities with advanced medical technology
    c. when people are prevented from taking barbiturates and similar drugs
    d. when people are given fresh milk to drink
    e. when people are exposed to ultraviolet radiation

17. In East Asia the development of _____, followed by the invention of _____ and a host of other things in China resulted in expansion of northern Chinese populations and displacements of southern Chinese peoples into southeast Asia.
    a. herding/iron
    b. irrigation/the printing press
    c. farming/bronze
    d. armies/gunpowder
    e. a religious hierarchy/the rudder

18. In the United States, the idea of race originated in the _____century to refer to the diverse peoples—European settlers, conquered Indians and Africans imported as slaves—that were brought together in colonial North America.
    a. seventeenth
    b. sixteenth
    c. nineteenth
    d. eighteenth
    e. fifteenth

19. Studies of body build and climatic adaptation are complicated by the intervening effects on physique of diet, since dietary differences will cause variation in body build. Another complicating factor is _____. Thus, much of the way humans adapt to cold is cultural, rather biological.
    a. furniture.
    b. housing.
    c. availability of water.
    d. energy.
    e. clothes.

20. A number of studies involving identical twins have appeared to indicate an appreciable degree of hereditary control of intelligence. There are, however, enormous problems in attempting to separate genetic components from environmental factors. Which of the following would be considered problematic with the findings from twin studies?
    a. failure to make sure "'separated twins\rdblquote really were raised separately
    b. untested assumptions about similarity of environments
    c. inadequate sample sizes
    d. biased subjective judgements
    e. all of the above

21. The forces responsible for the considerable physical variation from one population to another include:
    a. the sexual attractiveness of potential partners.
    b. the promiscuity of males.
    c. genetic drift.
    d. biological adaptation to differing climates.
    e. *c* and *d*.

22. Up until 6000 the _____ in humans permitted efficient storage of fat to draw on in times of food shortage, and in times of scarcity conserved glucose for use in brain and red blood cells, as well as nitrogen through its diminished exertion.
    a. thrifty hormones
    b. non-thrifty genotype
    c. liberal genotype
    d. conservative genotype
    e. thrifty genotype

Answers to multiple-choice practice questions

1. d	7. c	13. b	18. d
2. c	8. b	14. e	19. e
3. c	9. e	15. a	20. e
4. b	10. e	16. b	21. e
5. d	11. b	17. c	22. e
6. e	12. d		

True/False Practice Questions

1. A species in the gene pool of which there are alternative forms (alleles) for particular genes is called *polymorphic*.

2. Epicanthic eye folds are most common in Caucasian populations.

3. Lactose-intolerance is a characteristic of 80% of people of European descent.

4. Haviland is critical of the practice of shipping powdered milk supplements as foreign aid.

5. In Europe the east-west gradient in the frequency of Type B blood contrasts with the north-south gradient in skin color.

Answers to true/false practice questions

1. F   2. F   3. F   4. T   5. T

Practice Essay

1. Trace the historical development of race classification schemes, discussing their problems and limitations. What is the proper use of the term "race" today?

2. There are at least 51 chemicals, many of them in common use, now known to disrupt hormones. How do they do this? What are the effects of such disruptions?

Chapter 14
The Nature of Culture

Synopsis

In Chapter 14 the author considers the concept of culture, which underlies the anthropological enterprise. He proposes possible avenues for the definition of culture and describes how anthropologists attempt to study culture in the field. Finally, he raises questions as to whether it is possible for anthropologists to evaluate and compare cultures.

What you should learn from this chapter

1. Understand what culture is.
2. Know how culture is transmitted along generations.
3. Know how anthropologists conduct research into cultures.
4. Understand how culture functions in society.
5. Understand the relationship between culture and adaptation.

Key Terms and Names

culture

society

social structure

gender

subcultures

pluralistic societies

enculturation

Leslie White

A. R. Radcliffe-Brown

integration

adaptation

Bronislaw Malinowski

ethnocentrism

cultural relativism

structural-functionalism

symbol

Review Questions

1. What are four characteristics of culture, according to Haviland?

2. Distinguish between "culture" and "society." Do they always go together?

3. Distinguish between sex and gender.

4. Give an example of a pluralistic society, and consider what factors seem to allow the larger culture to tolerate subcultural variation.

5. How is culture passed on?

6. What is meant by the "integration" of various aspects of culture? Give an example.

7. How was anthropology able to contribute to the architectural problems of the Apache Indians?

8. What are three ways in which anthropologists should obtain data in another culture, according to the text?

9. How did Malinowski define the "needs" to be fulfilled by all cultures?

10. What did Annette Weiner find out about Trobriand women?

11. How do the Yanomami adapt to their sociopolitical environment?

12. What five functions must a culture serve, according to your text?

13. What changes have recently impacted many pastoralists in sub-Saharan Africa?

14. In what ways must a balance be struck between society and the individuals who comprise it?

15. How can the large-scale sacrifices of the Aztec be explained?

16. Distinguish between ethnocentrism and cultural relativism.

17. According to Walter Goldschmidt, what aspects of society indicate how well the physical and psychological needs of its people are being met?

18. What was E. B. Tylor's original definition of culture in 1871? (This is a classic definition in anthropology, so it would be worthwhile to become familiar with it.)

19. Approximately how old is human culture?

Fill-in-the-Blank

1. The culture concept was first developed in the _____ century.

2. Haviland defines culture as "a set of _____ shared by members of a society that when acted upon by the members of a society, produce behavior that falls within a range of variance the members consider proper and acceptable."

3. When groups function within a society with their own distinctive standards of behavior, we speak of _____ variation.

4. Enculturation refers to the process through which culture is transmitted from one _____ to the next.

5. According to anthropologist _____, all human behavior originates in the use of symbols.

6. Radcliffe-Brown was the originator of a school of thought known as _____.

7. In Kapauku culture, gardens of _____ supply most of the food, but it is through breeding pigs that a man achieves political power.

8. There is a difference between what people say the rules are and actual behavior; that is, the anthropologist must distinguish between the _____ and the real.

9. Inheritance among the Trobrianders is carried through the _____ line.

10. Most organisms adapt by acquiring changes in their _____.

11. Pastoral nomadic people in Africa south of the _____ have survived droughts because of their mobility.

12. The members of all societies consider their own culture to be the best; thus all people can be said to be _____.

13. Anthropology tries to promote cultural _____ or the idea that a culture must be evaluated according to its own standards.

Exercise

Briefly identify the cultures listed below and locate them on the world map.

1. Amish   2. Kapauku Papuans

3. Trobrianders   4. Apache

Multiple-Choice Practice Questions

1. The contemporary definition of culture has changed from the meaning given to it during the nineteenth century. Today,
   a. culture is seen as values and beliefs that lie behind behavior rather than as actual behavior.
   b. culture is seen as real rather than as ideal.
   c. the term "culture" has been replaced by the term "society."
   d. culture is defined as objects rather than ideas.
   e. the term "culture" is not used.

2. One way to determine if people share the same culture is to observe whether they
   a. are dependent on each other for survival.
   b. are able to interpret and predict each other's actions.
   c. live in the same territory.
   d. behave in an identical manner.
   e. All of the above

3. Which of the following statements about society and culture is INCORRECT?
   a. Culture can exist without a society.
   b. A society can exist without culture.
   c. Ants and bees have societies but no culture.
   d. A culture is shared by the members of a society.
   e. Although members of a society may share a culture, their behavior is not uniform.

4. Every culture teaches its members that there are differences between people based on sex, age, occupation, class, and ethnic group. People learn to predict the behavior of people playing different roles from their own. This means that
   a. culture is shared even though everyone is not the same.
   b. everyone plays the same role.
   c. all cultures identify the same roles.
   d. all cultures require that their participants play different roles, even though that means that no one can predict the behavior of others.
   e. everyone plays the same role throughout his or her life.

5. The cultural definitions of what it means to be a male or female today
   a. are determined by biological differences.
   b. are independent of biological differences.
   c. stem from biological differences that today are relatively insignificant.
   d. developed about 60 million years ago.
   e. have no relationship to sex.

6. When groups function within a society with their own distinctive standards of behavior, we speak of
   a. subcultural variation.
   b. social structure.
   c. gender differences.
   d. cultural materialism
   e. ethnocentrism.

7. The Amish may be used as an example of a/an
    a. pluralistic society.
    b. subculture.
    c. integrated society.
    d. world culture.
    e. complex society.

8. The process by which culture is transmitted from one generation to the next is
    a. enculturation.
    b. pluralism.
    c. adaptation.
    d. cultural relativism.
    e. subcultural variation.

9. Which of the following statements is INCORRECT?
    a. All culture is learned.
    b. All learned behavior is cultural.
    c. Culture is humankind's "social heredity."
    d. Culture is not biologically inherited.
    e. The process whereby culture is transmitted from one generation to the next is called enculturation.

10. The most important symbolic aspect of culture is
    a. art.
    b. language.
    c. religion.
    d. money.
    e. politics.

11. Among the Kapauku Papuans of New Guinea, the fact that an attempt to eliminate warfare (which would create a balanced sex ratio) would affect the practice of polygyny, which would affect the economy (since women raise pigs, and the more wives a man has the more pigs he can keep), shows that culture is
    a. materialistic.
    b. relative.
    c. pluralistic.
    d. integrated.
    e. enculturated.

12. An anthropologist develops a concept of culture by considering which of the following sources of data from the field?
    a. what people say they ought to do
    b. how people think they are behaving in accordance with these rules
    c. what people actually do
    d. All of the above
    e. None of the above

13. When Annette Weiner went to the Trobriand Islands sixty years after Malinowski had been there, she found that
    a. the culture had changed so much that it was almost unrecognizable.
    b. Malinowski's views of wealth, political power, and descent were primarily from the male's point of view.
    c. Malinowski had attributed power to women that did not exist.
    d. only women were significant producers of wealth.
    e. women played no role in producing wealth.

14. The process by which organisms adjust beneficially to their environment, or the characteristics by which they overcome hazards and gain access to the resources they need to survive, is called
    a. culture.
    b. biology.
    c. social structure.
    d. integration.
    e. adaptation.

15. Behavior can be adaptive in the short run but maladaptive in the long run. In the Central Valley in California, vast irrigation projects have created a garden, but salts and chemicals accumulating in the soil will eventually create another desert. This same process occurred in
    a. Mexico.
    b. Morocco.
    c. ancient Mesopotamia.
    d. Great Britain.
    e. the Yellow River valley of China.

16. A culture must satisfy basic needs such as
    a. the distribution of necessary goods and services.
    b. biological continuity through reproduction and enculturation of functioning adults.
    c. maintenance of order within a society and between a society and outsiders.
    d. motivation to survive.
    e. All of the above

17. According to Leslie White, which of the following is a symbol?
    a. a painting
    b. a novel
    c. walking across an intersection
    d. brushing your teeth
    e. All of the above

18. _____ refers to the position that because cultures are unique, each one can be evaluated according to its own standards and values.
    a. Ethnocentrism
    b. Cultural relativism
    c. Cultural materialism
    d. Adaptation
    e. Pluralism

19. Goldschmidt suggests that it is possible to decide which cultures are more successful than others by looking at which ones
    a. survive.
    b. last the longest.
    c. satisfy the physical and cultural needs of the people.
    d. support the most people.
    e. are the least emotional.

20. When anthropologist _____ observed that all human behavior originates in the use of symbols, he expressed an opinion shared by all anthropologists.
    a. Alfred Kroeber
    b. E. E. Evans-Pritchard
    c. Francis Shu
    d. A. F. C. Wallace
    e. Leslie White

21. A mountain people of western New Guinea studied in 1955 by the North American anthropologist Leo Pospisil.
    a. !Kung San
    b. Kaluli
    c. Basseri
    d. Kapauku
    e. Azande

22. We now know that any culture that is functioning adequately regards itself as the best, a view reflecting a phenomenon known as _____
    a. cultural relatvism.
    b. egoism.
    c. nationalistic.
    d. ethnocentrism.
    e. individualism.

23. The idea that one must suspend judgment on other peoples' practices in order to understand them in their own cultural terms is called _____
    a. structuralism.
    b. functionalism.
    c. structural functionalism.
    d. cultural relativism.
    e. relative culturalism.

24. In regards to the concept of cultural relativism, anthropologist _____ emphasized that ". . . one does not avoid making judgements, but rather postpones them in order to make informed judgements later."
    a. David Maybury-Lewis
    b. Daniel Day-Lewis
    c. Francis L. K. Shu
    d. E. E. Evans-Pritchard
    e. A. F. C. Wallace

25. As a result of _____ work, in 1981, the Apaches were able to move into houses that had been designed with *their* participation, for *their* specific needs.
    a. Walter Goldschmidt's
    b. George Esber's
    c. David Maybury-Lewis's
    d. Bronislaw Malinowski's
    e. Margaret Mead's

26. The British anthropologist _____ was the originator of what has come to be known as the structural-functionalist school of thought.
    a. Claude Levi-Strauss
    b. George Simmel
    c. A. R. Radcliffe-Brown
    d. Leslie A. White
    e. Ruth Benedict

27. _____ was a major theoretician in North American anthropology who saw culture as consisting of three essential components, which he referred to as technoeconomic, the social, and the ideological.
    a. A. R. Radcliffe-Brown
    b. Leslie A. White
    c. Leopold Pospisil
    d. A. B. Weiner
    e. William Jankowiak

Answers to multiple-choice practice questions

1. a	8. a	15. c	22. d
2. b	9. b	16. e	23. d
3. a	10. b	17. e	24. a
4. a	11. d	18. b	25. b
5. c	12. d	19. c	26. c
6. a	13. b	20. e	27. b
7. b	14. e	21. d	

True/False Practice Questions

1. To say that culture is shared means that all members of a society behave in the same way.

2. A pluralistic society always has subcultural variation, but not every society with subcultural variation is pluralistic.

3. A larger culture is more likely to tolerate a subculture if their values and physical appearances are similar.

4. Cattle herding is the mainstay around which all of Kapauku Papuan society revolves.

5. A modern definition of culture emphasizes the values, beliefs, and rules that lie behind behavior rather than the actual observable behavior itself.

6. Gender differences were more extreme among food foragers than among late nineteenth- and early twentiety-century Westerners.

7. Annette Weiner agrees that ethnographic writing can never be more than a fictional account.

8. There are some societies that have no regulation of sex whatsoever.

9. There can be no culture without a society.

10. Ants and bees instinctively cooperate in a manner that clearly indicates a degree of social organization; therefore, they have culture.

11. Though one's sex is culturally determined, one's sexual identity or gender is biologically constructed.

12. The degree of tolerance accorded the Amish is due in part to the fact that they are "white" Europeans.

13. So-called racial characteristics represent biological adaptations to climate and have nothing to do with differences in intelligence or cultural superiority.

14. Learned behavior is exhibited to one degree or another by most, if not all, mammals.

15. If a society is to survive, it must succeed in balancing the self-interest of its members against the demands of the society as a whole.

16. Numerous studies by a variety of social scientists have clearly shown that the death penalty does deter violent crime in the United States.

17. Cross-cultural studies show that homicide rates mostly decline after the death penalty is abolished.

Answers to true/false practice questions

1. F	7. F	13. T
2. T	8. F	14. T
3. T	9. T	15. T
4. F	10. F	16. F
5. F	11. F	17. T
6. F	12. T	

Practice Matching

Match the culture with its description.

1. _____ Amish

2. _____ Trobrianders

3. _____ Kapauku Papuans

4. _____ Aztec

5. _____ Apache

a. A Native American people with distinct architectural needs

b. A Pacific Island people studied by both Bronislaw Malinowski and Annette Weiner

c. A pacifist agrarian subculture of the United States

d. A New Guinea people who breed pigs

e. A civilization in Mexico that engaged in large-scale sacrifices.

Answers to practice matching

1. c   2. b   3. d   4. e   5. a

Practice Essays

1. Using the Amish as an example of subcultural variation, discuss some of the factors that seem to determine whether or not subcultural variation is tolerated by the larger culture. Compare the Amish to another group that is less well tolerated.

2. Distinguish between the concepts of culture and society.

3. Discuss the distinction between sex and gender and explain why this distinction is important.

4. Discuss the interrelatedness of the various parts of Kapauku culture. Use examples.

5. Because of the male bias of his European culture, Bronislaw Malinowski's pioneering study of the Trobriand Islanders missed many important factors. Discuss the factors that were overlooked due to male bias.

6. Provide examples to support the statement, "What is adaptive in one context may be seriously maladaptive in another."

7. Using the example of the Kapauku Papuans, explain the idea that culture is integrated.

8. Anthropologist James Peacock wrote a book called *The Anthropological Lens* in which he compared culture to a lens or glass through which people experience the world. The anthropologist, then, is like an oculist who hopes to find the "formula" of each kind of lens, acquiring a kind of stereoscopy, or depth perception, by being able to perceive things through multiple lenses. How is culture like a lens? What are the limitations of this metaphor for understanding culture and anthropology?

9. Are animals other than humans capable of culture?

Chapter 15
Language and Communication

Synopsis

Chapter 15 introduces the field of anthropological linguistics, considering how existing languages are described and studied and what the history of language can tell us. It examines how language is related to culture and explores the evolution of the capacity for language. An extensive technical vocabulary relating to linguistics is presented.

What You Should Learn From This Chapter

1. Know how humans communicate with one another.
2. Know what linguistics is and the components of language.
3. Understand how humans use paralanguage to communicate.
4. Understand how humans use kinesics to communicate.
5. Know how ethnolinguistics aids in understanding culture.
6. Know the explanations offered about the origin of language.

Key Terms

language

symbol

signal

linguistics

phonetic

phonology

phonemes

morphemes

bound morphemes

free morpheme

frame substitution

syntax

grammar

form classes

kinesics

paralanguage

voice qualities

vocalizations

vocal characterizers

vocal qualifiers

vocal segregates

language family

linguistic divergence

glottochronology

core vocabulary

linguistic nationalism

ethnolinguistics

Sapir-Whorf hyothesis

dialects

sociolinguistics

code switching

displacement

Review Questions

1. Why is language so important to culture?

2. What is the anatomical "price we pay" for our vocal capabilities?

3. What does primatologist Allison Jolly mean by the "audience effect" she observes among the primates she studies?

4. Distinguish between a morpheme and a phonome, and give an example of each.

5. Distinguish between bound and free morphemes, and give examples of each.

6. What is the function of frame substitution?

7. What is the purpose of a form class?

8. What method does descriptive linguistics use?

9. What is paralanguage? Provide examples.

10. What are the characteristic differences in body posture between men and women?

11. What is the "gesture-call" system?

12. What are the elements of voice quality?

13. Distinguish between vocal characterizers and vocal qualifiers.

14. How are gender markers employed?

15. What is code switching? Give an example you have observed.

16. What does glottochronology seek to explain?

17. Describe the importance of language for group identity.

18. What does ethnolinguistics seek to explain?

19. Provide an example that would support the Sapir-Whorf hypothesis.

20. What is meant by color-naming behavior?

21. How can linguistics use metaphor as a key to understanding culture?

22. Why do linguists study kinship terms?

23. Haviland notes that wild speculation about the origins of language is no longer necessary. What advances have been made that make such speculation unnecessary?

24. What types of communication have primates been taught?

25. What are the communicative capabilities of monkeys and apes?

26. What is the difference between a signal and a symbol?

Fill-in-the-Blank

1. There are about _____ languages in the world.

2. A symbol has an arbitrary meaning determined by cultural convention, while a _____ has a natural or self-evident meaning.

3. Of all the potential sounds that can be made by the human vocal system, no more than _____ are used by any particular language.

4. The modern scientific study of language by Europeans began in the _____ with the collection of information about exotic languages by European explorers, invaders, and missionaries.

5. _____ is the systematic study of the production, transmission, and reception of speech sounds.

6. The smallest class of sound that makes a difference in meaning is called a _____.

7. The smallest significant unit of sound that carries a meaning is called a _____.

8. The entire formal structure of a language is called its _____.

9. The method used to define the rules and regularities of a language is called frame _____.

10. _____ refers to the extralinguistic noises that accompany language.

11. _____ are the background characteristics of a speaker's voice that convey the state of the speaker.

12. Sounds such as "shh" and "uh-huh" that are similar to speech sounds but do not appear in sequences that can be called words are vocal _____.

13. _____ is usually referred to as "body language."

14. _____ linguistics studies relationships between earlier and later languages.

15. English belongs to the _____ language family.

16. Linguistic _____ refers to the attempt by nations to proclaim their independence and distinctive identity by celebrating their own language.

17. The study of the relationship between language and social factors is called _____.

18. The process by which a person changes from one level of language to another is called _____.

Multiple-Choice Practice Questions

1. A system of communication based on symbols is called a
   a. signal.
   b. form class.
   c. language.
   d. frame substitution.
   e. vocalization.

2. All languages are organized on the same basic plan in that
   a. they are all based on signals.
   b. they take no more than fifty sounds and put them together in meaningful ways according to rules that can be determined by linguists.
   c. they take no more than three thousand sounds and organize them according to the rules of grammar.
   d. they all evolved from a common Egyptian language.
   e. they originated in Russia.

3. The modern scientific study of all aspects of language is
   a. kinesics.
   b. phonology.
   c. linguistics.
   d. grammar.
   e. glottochronology.

4. The systematic study of the production, transmission, and reception of speech sounds is _____
   a. linguistics.
   b. morphology.
   c. frame substitution.
   d. phonetics.
   e. syntax.

5. Paralanguage is to speech as _____ is to position of the body.
   a. kinesics
   b. ethnolinguistics
   c. form class
   d. phonetics
   e. displacement

6. Consider the English word "dog." Which of the following is a morpheme?
   a. "d"
   b. "dog"
   c. "o"
   d. "g"
   e. all of the above

7. The sounds *s* and *z* in "cats" and "dogs" are examples of
   a. allphones.
   b. allomorphs.
   c. free morphemes.
   d. bound morphemes.
   e. signals.

8. The method called frame substitution enables the linguist to establish the rules or principles by which language users construct phrases and sentences, that is, the _____ of the language.
   a. morphology
   b. form classes
   c. core vocabulary
   d. sociolinguistics
   e. syntax

9. Two people say to you, "You sure look nice today." Although they are saying the same words, you can tell that one person is being complementary and the other sarcastic by their
   a. vocalizations.
   b. vocal characteristics.
   c. voice qualities.
   d. voice segregates.
   e. vocal qualifiers.

10. Kinesics is a method for notating and analyzing
    a. screaming.
    b. kissing.
    c. any form of body "language."
    d. fighting.
    e. food.

11. Descriptive linguistics
    a. attempts to explain the features of a particular language at one time in its history.
    b. looks at languages as separate systems without considering how they might be related to each other.
    c. attempts to construct a language's historical development.
    d. investigates relationships between earlier and later forms of the same language.
    e. *a* and *b* only

12. A language family is a group of languages that
    a. all have the same core vocabulary.
    b. are subordinate to a dominant language.
    c. all have the same syntax.
    d. use the same number of sounds.
    e. are descended from a single ancestral language.

13. If the core vocabulary of two languages is compared by glottochronologists, it is thought possible to determine
    a. if the two languages perceive reality in the same way.
    b. if the two languages use the same syntax.
    c. if they share the same allophones.
    d. if they have a similar technology.
    e. how long ago the languages separated from each other.

14. Which of the following statements about linguistic divergence is INCORRECT?
    a. One force for linguistic change is borrowing by one language from another.
    b. If languages were isolated from each other, there would be very little linguistic change.
    c. New vocabulary emerges in a language due to the quest for novelty and the development of specialized vocabulary by groups.
    d. Changes in pronunciation may emerge as markers of class boundary (e.g., upper-class "U" vs. "Non-U").
    e. Dying languages may be revived in the name of linguistic nationalism.

15. Which of the following is NOT an example of linguistic nationalism?
    a. You are a Spanish-speaking person in the United States and want your children to learn English so that they can assimilate more completely into the society around them.
    b. A national committee in France declares that certain widely used terms will no longer be allowed to appear in public print because they are not French.
    c. You live in Scotland and are so alarmed by the rapid decline in the number of people speaking Gaelic that you start a school in which all subjects are taught in Gaelic.
    d. The southern part of India declares itself a separate country called Tamiland (the land of the people who speak Tami) in defiance of India's declaration of Hindi as the national language; people say they will die in defense of their "mother tongue."
    e. A country previously colonized by the British passes a law requiring everyone to speak the native tongue; English is banned because of its association with colonial domination.

16. The influence of a person's class status on what pronunciation he/she uses; a speaker's choice of more complicated vocabulary and grammar when he/she is speaking to a professional audience; the influence of language on culture—all these are the concerns of
    a. descriptive linguistics.
    b. historical linguistics.
    c. ethnolinguistics.
    d. linguistic nationalism.
    e. displacement.

17. Which of the following statements about the Sapir-Whorf hypothesis is INCORRECT?
    a. It was first formulated by Edward Sapir and Benjamin Whorf.
    b. It may be briefly explained with the sentence "Language determines the reality that speakers of the language perceive."
    c. It may be briefly explained with the sentence "Language reflects reality; it only mirrors what people perceive."
    d. It is expressed in this example: If in a factory a metal drum is labeled "empty" (when in fact it is filled with flammable fumes), people will perceive it as empty and may do things with it that may create a fire hazard (such as storing it near a furnace); but if it is labeled "full" of gaseous fumes, people will perceive it as a fire hazard and treat it more carefully.
    e. none of the above

18. The term _____ is usually used to refer to varying forms of a language that reflect particular regions or social classes and that are similar enough to be mutually intelligible.
    a. dialect
    b. language subgroup
    c. language family
    d. linguistic nationalism
    e. Sapir-Whorf hypothesis

19. On April 10, 1984, the _____ became the first community of Native Americans in the United States to affirm the right of its members to regain and maintain fluency in the ancestral language.
    a. Southern Paiute
    b. Northern Paiute
    c. Northern Ute
    d. Isleta Pueblo
    e. Apache

20. The very names for this dialect reflect the diversity of views. Which of the following are NOT terms used to refer to Ebonics.
    a. African American English (AAE)
    b. African American Vernacular English (AAVE)
    c. Black English (BE)
    d. African American Dialect (AAD)
    e. *a* and *d*

21. Which of the following is NOT true of Black English?
    a. It has a short history.
    b. It has logical rules of grammar.
    c. Its discourse practices cannot be traced.
    d. It has an oral literature worthy of respect.
    e. *a* and *c*

Answers to multiple-choice practice questions

1. c	7. d	13. e	19. c
2. b	8. e	14. b	20. e
3. c	9. c	15. a	21. e
4. d	10. c	16. c	
5. a	11. e	17. c	
6. b	12. e	18. a	

True/False Practice Questions

1. Haviland traces linguistics back to the ancient grammarians in China more than three thousand years ago.

2. Glottochronology assumes that the rate at which a language's core vocabulary changes is variable and thus cannot be used to give an exact date for when two languages diverged.

3. According to the hypothesis devised by Sapir and Whorf, if you had only one word to describe what English speakers call "red" and "yellow," you would not be likely to perceive the shades of red and yellow in a sunset.

4. Though men and women in North American culture typically utilize slightly different vocabularies, the body language they use does not differ much.

5. The emphasis on the French language by Quebecois separatists is an example of linguistic nationalism.

6. "Ebonics" is a substandard or defective dialect of English.

7. The Oakland Public Schools wanted to teach Black English in its schools.

8. There was a sense of outrage among some that a stigmatized variety of English would be treated as a valid way of talking in the Oakland Public Schools.

9. There is really very little difference between Black English (BE) and Standard English (SE).

10. The Oakland school board wrongfully concluded that teachers needed to understand the differences between Standard English and Black English to properly teach children.

11. Black English is not just some random form of "broken-down English" intrinsically inferior to Standard English but is a speech variety with its own long history.

12. The problem with Black English is that its rules of grammar are illogical.

13. Black English has discourse practices traceable to West African languages and a vibrant oral literature worthy of respect.

14. In general, Black English has not added much to the vocabulary of American English.

15. A major criticism of the Oakland School Board's proposal to teach Ebonics is that teachers would be wasting time "teaching" African American Vernacular English when kids should be learning Standard English.

16. According to linguistic anthropologist Ron Kephart, the most important work that anthropologists and linguists have to do is to raise public awareness and understanding of what linguistic, cultural, and biological differences mean and, most important, what they don't mean.

17. What the Oakland School Board proposed in regard to teaching Ebonics is no different from what is being done, with considerable success, in several other countries.

Answers to true/false practice questions

1. F	6. F	11. T	16. T
2. F	7. F	12. F	17. T
3. T	8. T	13. T	
4. F	9. F	14. F	
5. T	10. F	15. T	

Practice Matching

Match the term to its definition.

1. _____ bound morpheme

2. _____ phonemes

3. _____ form classes

4. _____ kinesics

5. _____ glottochronology

a. A method of dating divergence within language families

b. The smallest classes of sound that make a difference in meaning

c. A sound that occurs in a language only in combination with other sounds, as *s* in English to signify the plural

d. Postures, facial expressions, and body motion

e. The parts of speech that work the same in any sentence.

Answers to practice matching

1. c   2. b   3. e   4. d   5. a

Practice Essays

1. Would it be accurate to claim language as a distinguishing feature of *Homo sapiens?*

2. How is language linked to gender? Use examples from the text and add some of your own.

3. Discuss the "Great Ebonics Controversy." What are the arguments of the proponents of Ebonics? What are the arguments of those who oppose Ebonics?

4. What was the Northern Ute Language Renewal Project?

Chapter 16
Growing Up Human

Synopsis

Chapter 16 focuses on how culture is transmitted from one generation to the next and explores the cultural contexts in which personalities are formed. It suggests a relativistic understanding of normality and abnormality and looks at recent changes in the field of psychological anthropology.

What you should learn from this chapter

1. Understand the process and agents of enculturation.
2. Understand how the behavioral environment functions.
3. Understand how personality is shaped.
4. Understand the concepts of dependence and independence training in child rearing.
5. Know how group personality is determined.
6. Understand the purpose and criticism of national character studies.
7. Know how normality and abnormality are defined.

Key Terms and Names

enculturation

self-awareness

patterns of affect

personality

Margaret Mead

dependence training

independence training

group personality

modal personality

national character

Ruth Fulton Benedict

core values

mental illness

ethnic psychoses

Review Questions

1. Who are the agents of enculturation?

2. What are three aspects of self-awareness, according to Haviland?

3. Why might North American children's motor development lag behind that of children from non-Western societies?

4. What are three aspects of the behavioral environment?

5. What does the study of the Penobscot tell us about culture and personality?

6. Describe the situation of the Ju/'hoansi.

7. What did the Original Study of the Mbuti indicate about child-rearing patterns?

8. Distinguish between dependence and independence training.

9. What did Margaret Mead's study of adolescent Samoans tell us?

10. Provide an example of modal personality.

11. Explain the basic statistics behind the concept of modal personality.

12. What purpose do the Rorschach and Thematic Apperception Tests serve?

13. What does Francis Hsu suggest are major personality traits of the Chinese?

14. What problems accompany the use of modal personality assessment?

15. What contribution did Ruth Benedict make to the field of culture and personality?

16. Why were national character studies undertaken?

17. What was Gorer's toilet-training hypothesis?

18. What are the major objections to national character studies?

19. Provide examples of core values.

20. What is the function of the *two-spirit* in Plains Indians society?

21. How are male and female role identities shaped by the structure of the human family, according to Nancy Chodorow?

22. How is abnormal behavior defined?

23. How are cures effected among the Melemchi of Nepal?

24. What is "windigo"?

Fill-in-the-Blank

1. The Enlightenment thinker John Locke presented the concept of _____ to express the idea that humans are born as "blank slates" and that everything depends on experience.

2. The term _____ refers to the process by which culture is transmitted from one generation to the next.

3. The Penobscot traditionally conceived of the self as divided into two parts, the body and the _____.

4. Margaret Mead studied three societies in _____ and found out that sex roles were highly variable.

5. Margaret Mead was a founder of the field called _____.

6. The Ju/'hoansi made a living by _____ in the Kalahari Desert.

7. A concept that attempted to retain the idea of a group personality and yet take into account the diversity of personalities within a group is the concept of _____.

8. The ink-blot test is properly called the _____ test.

9. The studies developed during World War II to explore the idea that modern nations could be characterized by personality types were called _____ studies.

10. The psychosis exhibited by northern Algonkian Indian groups who recognize the existence of cannibalistic monsters is called _____.

Exercise

Briefly identify the cultures listed below, and locate them on the world map.

1. Penobscot

2. Arapesh, Mundugamor, Tchambuli

3. Ju/'hoansi

4. Mbuti

5. Yanomami

6. Dobu

7. Melemchi

8. Algonkian Indians

Multiple-Choice Practice Questions

1. Enculturation is the process of transmitting
   a. society from one generation to the next.
   b. social norms from one adult to another.
   c. culture from one child to another.
   d. culture from one generation to the next.
   e. personality from parent to child.

2. The agents of enculturation
   a. are persons involved in transmitting culture to the next generation.
   b. are at first the members of the family into which the child is born.
   c. vary, depending on the structure of the family into which a child is born.
   d. include peer groups and schoolteachers.
   e. All of the above

3. Which of the following statements about self-awareness is INCORRECT?
   a. Self-awareness occurs earlier in children as a function of the amount of social stimulation they receive.
   b. At fifteen weeks of age, the home-reared infant in North America is in contact with its mother for about 20 percent of time.
   c. At fifteen weeks of age, infants in the Ju/'hoansi society of South Africa's Kalahari Desert are in close contact with their mothers about 70 percent of the time.
   d. American children develop self-awareness earlier than do Ju/'hoansi children.
   e. All of the above are correct.

4. The _____ includes definitions and explanations of objects, spatial orientation, and temporal orientation, as well as culturally defined values, ideals, and standards that provide an individual with a normative orientation.
   a. vital self
   b. *tabula rasa*
   c. behavioral environment
   d. patterns of affect
   e. core values

5. In studying three societies in New Guinea, Margaret Mead found that the role played by men and women were determined primarily by
   a. genes.
   b. biology.
   c. culture.
   d. incest.
   e. the food they ate.

6. Margaret Mead's groundbreaking work in culture and personality published in 1928 was a deliberate test of a Western psychological hypothesis. What was this hypothesis?
   a. Lowering the drinking age will promote promiscuity.
   b. Child-rearing practices have no effect on adult personality.
   c. The stress and conflict experienced by American adolescents is a universal phenomenon based on maturing hormones.
   d. By changing child-rearing practices, we can change the structure of society.
   e. By lowering the driving age, we can promote less stress among adolescents.

7. A study of child rearing among the Ju/'hoansi of Africa indicates that
   a. boys and girls are raised in a very similar manner and are both mild-mannered and self-reliant.
   b. because girls are out gathering most of the time, they are expected to be more aggressive and self-reliant than boys are.
   c. mothers spend the least amount of time with their children, and thus the children identify strongly with their fathers.
   d. boys do more work than girls.
   e. boys have less responsibility than girls and get to play more of the time.

8. Independence training, according to Child and Whitings, is more likely in
   a. small nuclear families.
   b. large extended families.
   c. small-scale horticultural societies where a man has many wives.
   d. a pastoralist family where a woman has many husbands and the extended family has to be always on the move.
   e. New York City neighborhoods where large families stay nearby and support each other.

9. Dependence training is more likely in
   a. nuclear families.
   b. societies whose subsistence is based on pastoralism.
   c. a food-foraging society.
   d. extended families in societies whose economy is based on subsistence farming.
   e. industrial societies.

10. The personality typical of a society, as indicated by the central tendency of a defined frequence distribution, is called
    a. core values.
    b. nuclear personality.
    c. patterns of affect..
    d. culture and personality
    e. modal personality.

11. Which of the following statements about modal personality is INCORRECT?
    a. Although a modal personality may be found for a particular society, a range of personalities may exist in that society.
    b. Although the modal personality may be considered "normal" for that society, it may be shared by less than half of the population.
    c. Those who study modal personality accept the fact that there may be abnormal individuals in that society.
    d. Data on modal personality are usually gathered by the use of psychological tests such as the Rorschach and TAT.
    e. All of the above are correct

12. Studies of _____ were developed during World War II to explore the idea that basic personality traits were shared by most of the people in modern nations.
    a. modal personality
    b. national character
    c. stereotype
    d. group personality
    e. independence training

13. The term "core values" refers to
    a. those aspects of culture that pertain to the way a culture makes its living.
    b. rules that guide family and home life.
    c. those values emphasized by a particular culture.
    d. common shares in Golden Delicious Corp.
    e. the beliefs stressed by a particular political party.

14. Among the Plains Indians, a man who wore women's clothes, performed women's work, and married another man
    a. was considered normal.
    b. was sought out as a curer, artist, and matchmaker.
    c. was assumed to have great spiritual power.
    d. might have been homosexual.
    e. All of the above

15. An ethnic psychosis refers to a
    a. psychotic episode experienced by a person from an exotic culture.
    b. progressive disease that strikes anthropologists when they spend more than twelve months in the field.
    c. psychosis characterized by symptoms peculiar to a particular group.
    d. universal form of mental illness.
    e. biologically based disease that resembles schizophrenia.

16. Traditional culture and personality studies
    a. were important in undermining ethnocentrism.
    b. are criticized today for being impressionistic and difficult to replicate.
    c. diversified the study of psychological processes in a cultural context.
    d. promoted a relativistic point of view.
    e. All of the above

17. According to your textbook, among the Yanomami
    a. all men are fierce and warlike.
    b. all men are quiet and retiring.
    c. there is a range of personalities.
    d. a quiet, retiring Yanomamo would not survive.
    e. a fierce, warlike Yanomamo would not survive.

18. When Mbuti children enter the *bopi* or playground, the most important principle guiding their social interaction is their
    a. gender.
    b. age.
    c. kinship relations.
    d. class status.
    e. caste status.

19. As _____ pioneering studies suggested, whatever biological differences may exist between men and women, they are extremely malleable.
    a. Ruth Benedict's
    b. Karen Sacks's
    c. Deborah Tannen's
    d. Margaret Mead's
    e. Laura Nader's

20. One of the "founding mothers" of anthropology is _____.
    a. Nancy Scheper-Hughes
    b. Catherine Bateson
    c. Mary Douglas
    d. Margaret Mead
    e. Emily Schultz

21. Today in Native American societies the preferred term to describe an individual who falls between the categories of "man" and "woman" is known as _____.
    a. berdache.
    b. gay.
    c. passive homosexual.
    d. two-spirit.
    e. effeminate.

Answers to multiple-choice practice questions

1. d	7. a	13. c	19. d
2. e	8. a	14. e	20. d
3. d	9. d	15. c	21. d
4. c	10. e	16. e	
5. c	11. e	17. c	
6. c	12. b	18. b	

True/False Practice Questions

1. What is considered "normal" in a society is defined by culture.

2. Anthropologists believe that all mental illness is learned rather than biologically based.

3. Both hunting and gathering societies and industrial societies promote independence training in their mobile nuclear families.

4. Margaret Mead believed that male and female roles were by and large defined by the biological attributes of the sexes.

5. National character studies were developed during World War II to explore the idea that basic personality traits were shared by most of the people in modern nations.

6. The primary contribution of Whiting and Child to the field of psychological anthropology was their in-depth study of the Ju/'hoansi.

7. The Yanomami of Brazil are known for their "fierceness," yet there is a range of personality types even there.

8. The Native American view sees intersexed individuals in a very positive and affirming light.

9. The Euro-American view of intersexed individuals is similar to the Native American view.

10. The extent to which Native Americans see spirituality is reflected in their belief that all things have spirit.

11. From the Native American perspective the spirit of a human is superior to the spirit of any other thing.

12. To Native Americans the function of religion is not to try to condemn or to change what exists, but to accept the realities of the world and to appreciate their contributions to life.

13. Native Americans believe everything that exists has a purpose.

14. An intersexed child is derided and viewed as a "freak of nature" in traditional Native American culture.

Answers to true/false practice questions.

1. T	6. F	11. F
2. F	7. T	12. T
3. T	8. T	13. T
4. F	9. F	14. F
5. T	10. T	

Practice Essays

1. Psychiatrist Thomas Szasz, in a book called *The Myth of Mental Illness,* described our society's medicalization of deviance, claiming that the decision to label a person as mentally ill is tied to the social, economic, and political order rather than to some absolute definition of sanity or normalcy. Is this an idea that anthropologists would be comfortable with? Can you compare this with any other examples of the social context of normality/abnormality discussed in the chapter?

2. What was the impact of Freudian psychoanalysis on the development of psychological anthropology? How have culture-and-personality specialists responded to the Freudian paradigm?

3. What is the traditional Penobscot concept of self? What did it have to do with their behavioral environment?

4. The author of the original study The Blessed Curse mentioned, "from a very early age I was presented with two different and conflicting views of myself." What did the author mean by this? Explain.

5. Explain why the Native American and Euro-American views on intersexuality are so diametrically opposed.

6. Discuss the importance of child-rearing practices for the development of gender-related personality characteristics. Provide examples.

7. Explain why child-rearing practices in the United States creates problems of gender identity for both sexes, although a different sort for each sex.

8. How does a culture itself induce certain kinds of psychological conflicts that have important consequences for the entire society?

Chapter 17
Patterns of Subsistence

Synopsis

In Chapter 17 the text examines the impact that various modes of subsistence have on cultures. Food foraging is described in detail, and the variations in food production systems are discussed.

What You Should Learn From This Chapter

1. Understand the role of adaptation in cultural survival:
   - unit of adaptation
   - evolutionary adaptation
   - culture areas
   - culture core
2. Understand the food-foraging way of life:
   - subsistence and sex roles
   - food sharing
   - cultural adaptations and material technology
   - egalitarian society
3. Understand food-producing society:
   - horticulturalist
   - pastoralist
   - intensive agriculture and preindustrial cities

Key Terms and Names

adaptation

horticulture

ecosystem

convergent evolution

parallel evolution

Julian Steward

culture area

culture type

cultural ecology

culture core

ethnoscientists

carrying capacity

density of social relations

pastoralist

swidden

preindustrial cities

Review Questions

1. What purpose does adaptation serve?

2. Describe the relationship the Tsembaga have with the environment.

3. Explain what is meant by a unit of adaptation.

4. What are human ecologists concerned with?

5. Describe Comanche adaptation to the plains environment.

6. Distinguish between convergent and parallel evolution.

7. Provide an example of how a culture can be stable while not necessarily static.

8. Use the Gururumba to illustrate horticulture as an adaptive pattern of subsistence.

9. Why did native groups on the plains not farm?

10. What is the role of the ethnoscientist?

11. About how many people currently live by food foraging?

12. What previously held misconceptions of food foragers have been refuted?

13. What are the main social characteristics of food foragers?

14. What are the size-limiting factors in a foraging group?

15. What purpose does population redistribution serve for the Ju/'hoansi?

16. What impact does biological sex have on the division of labor?

17. How is the behavior of food-foraging groups reflected in their material culture?

18. Why are food foragers generally egalitarian?

19. Can we make any generalizations about the status of women in foraging societies?

20. How is territory conceptualized in foraging societies?

21. Define the concerns of Julian Steward's study of cultural ecology.

22. Distinguish between horticulturalists and intensive agriculturalists.

23. What are the basic features of pastoralist society?

24. Define "adaptation" and "ecosystem" and illustrate the relevance of these concepts with the example of pig sacrifices among the Tsembaga.

25. Why has slash-and-burn (swidden) come to be viewed negatively by many people today?

26. Describe the subsistence practices of the Mekranoti.

27. How did anthropologist Alan Kolata help the Aymara with their agricultural problems?

Fill-in-the-Blank

1. _____ is the process by which organisms modify and adjust to their environment and thereby survive more effectively.

2. The main animal raised by the Gururumba is _____.

3. When the Comanche migrated to the Great Plains, they found a new food source, the _____.

4. When several societies with different cultural backgrounds move into a new environment and develop similar adaptations, they represent the cultural equivalent of _____ evolution.

5. When several societies with very similar cultural backgrounds develop along similar lines, they represent the process of _____ evolution.

6. A geographic region in which a number of different societies follow a similar pattern of life is called a culture _____.

7. The various societies of the Great Plains had common religious rituals, such as _____.

8. The subfield within anthropology that studies the interaction of specific cultures with their environments is called _____.

9. The anthropologist who pioneered this subfield was _____.

10. _____ try to understand folk ideologies and how they help a group survive.

11. Humans lived using food foraging until about _____ years ago, when domestication of animals and plants began.

12. The Ju/'hoansi of the Kalahari Desert have been called "the original _____ society" because they work so few hours a week.

13. The number of people who can be supported by a certain technology is the _____ of the environment.

14. About _____ percent of the diet of most food foragers is gathered by women.

15. Increased food sharing appears to be related to a shift in food habits involving increased eating of _____ around two and a half million years ago.

16. Another name for slash-and-burn is _____ farming.

17. The Bakhtiari of the Zagros Mountains are _____ who migrate seasonally from one location to another.

18. City life is based on a subsistence pattern of _____.

19. The main city of the Aztecs was _____.

20. The anthropologist who helped the Aymara was _____.

Exercises

I. Complete the chart below, filling in examples of each type of subsistence and noting its general characteristics. You can use this to study from later.

PATTERNS OF SUBSISTENCE

Type	Example	Characteristics
Foraging		
Pastoralism		
Horticulture		
Agriculture		

II. Briefly identify the cultures listed below, and locate them on the world map.

1. Tsembaga

2. Comanche

3. Shoshone and Paiute

4. Hadza

5. Mekranoti

6. Gurumba

7. Bakhtiari

8. Aymara

Multiple-Choice Practice Questions

1. Adaptation refers to the
   a. process by which organisms modify and adjust to their environment and thereby survive more effectively.
   b. ability of one population to destroy another.
   c. borrowing of cultural material from another society.
   d. process by which living systems change from birth to death.
   e. effect of child-rearing practices on basic personality structure.

2. Before the arrival of horses and guns, the Comanche were food foragers in southern Idaho. Their skill as hunters was put to good use as they used these new tools to hunt buffalo on the Great Plains. The term used to refer to existing customs that by chance have potential for a new cultural adaptation is
   a. convergent evolution.
   b. divergent evolutions.
   c. ecosystem.
   d. parallel evolution.
   e. preadaptations.

3. The Comanche and the Cheyenne were quite different culturally until they moved out onto the Great Plains and made use of the horse to hunt buffalo and raid settled peoples. They then became more similar in cultural adaptations, a process called
   a. preadaptation.
   b. development of a culture area.
   c. convergent evolution.
   d. parallel evolution.
   e. an ecosystem.

4. Native American food foragers established a way of life in New England and southern Quebec that lasted about five thousand years. This is indicative of
   a. stagnation.
   b. failure to progress.
   c. genetic inferiority
   d. lack of innovation.
   e. effective cultural adaptation.

5. A culture type is defined by
   a. the geographic area in which a people live.
   b. the kind of technology that a group has to exploit a particular environment.
   c. contacts with other cultures.
   d. sharing the same values.
   e. sharing the same language.

6. A taboo against eating certain foods, the belief that only a chief has strong enough
   magic to plant apple trees and dispense them to his fellow villagers, and the number
   of hours a people work each day are examples of what could be considered part of
   a society's
   a. structural base.
   b. foundation.
   c. infrastructure.
   d. culture core
   e. none of the above

7. Which of the following research topics might be of interest to an ethnoscientist?
   a. How the allele responsible for sickle-cell anemia increases or decreases in certain
      cultural environments, such a horticultural vs. hunting-gathering.
   b. Similarities and differences in the farming patterns of Southwest Asia and
      Mesoamerica.
   c. The ways in which a group classifies and explains the world; for example, the
      Tsembaga avoid low-lying, marshy areas filled with mosquitoes that carry malaria
      because they believe that such areas are inhabited by red spirits who punish
      trespassers.
   d. Reconstruction and comparison of archaeological sites in similar geographic
      regions.
   e. all of the above

8. Some anthropologists refer to food foragers as "the original affluent society" because
   a. they manage to accumulate a lot of wealth.
   b. they occupy the most attractive environments with abundant food supply.
   c. they live in marginal areas and are very poor.
   d. they earn a good wage for all hours of work they put in each week.
   e. they work only twelve to nineteen hours a week for a comfortable, healthy life.

9. The groups referred to as food foragers must live where there are naturally available
   food sources; thus they
   a. remain in permanent settlements.
   b. move about once every ten years.
   c. move frequently.
   d. adopt farming whenever they can.
   e. prefer to live in cities.

10. The number and intensity of interactions among the members of a residential unit
    is called
    a. density of social relations.
    b. social interactionism.
    c. cultural ecology.
    d. carrying capacity.
    e. convergent evolution.

11. Which of the following is NOT one of the three elements of human social organization
    that developed with hunting?
    a. sexual division of labor
    b. aggressive behavior
    c. food sharing
    d. the camp site
    e. all of the above

12. In a food-foraging society, how do people store food for the future?
    a. They keep a surplus in stone cairns.
    b. They keep extra plants in large, circular yam houses.
    c. They hide meat in each individual family residence.
    d. They rely on the generosity of others to share food.
    e. They keep dried food in a common storage shed.

13. To say that food-foraging societies are egalitarian means that
    a. there are no status differences.
    b. the only status differences are age and sex.
    c. everyone is equal except women.
    d. men are usually subordinate to women.
    e. children are the center of community life.

14. Someone who uses irrigation, fertilizers, and the plow to produce food on large plots
    of land is known as a/an _____
    a. horticulturalists.
    b. intensive agriculturalist.
    c. pastoralists.
    d. hunter-gatherer.
    e. industrialist.

15. _____ are food producers who specialize in animal husbandry and who consider their way of life to be ideal and central to defining their identities.
    a. Food foragers
    b. Horticulturalists
    c. Intensive agriculturalists
    d. Pastoralists
    e. Industrialists

16. Aztec society in the sixteenth century
    a. was a stratified society based on achievement and education.
    b. was an urbanized society in which kinship played no role in determining status.
    c. was an industrial city-state.
    d. was invincible to Cortes' attack.
    e. none of the above

17. Which of the following statements about preindustrial cities is INCORRECT?
    a. Preindustrial cities have existed in some parts of the world for thousands of years.
    b. Preindustrial cities represent a stage of development in the progression of human culture toward industrial cities.
    c. Tenochtitlan, the capital of the Aztec empire, is a good example of a preindustrial city.
    d. Preindustrial cities have a diversified economy.
    e. Preindustrial cities are highly stratified.

18. This North American developed an approach that he called cultural ecology, that is, the interaction between specific cultures with their environments.
    a. Alan Kolata
    b. Leslie White
    c. Fred Plog
    d. Julian Steward
    e. Barbara Myerhoff

19. After three years of tending their gardens the Mekranoti are left with only _____.
    a. manioc
    b. sweet potatoes
    c. pineapple
    d. tobacco
    e. bananas

Answers to multiple-choice practice questions

1. a	6. d	11. b	16. e
2. e	7. c	12. d	17. b
3. c	8. e	13. b	18. d
4. e	9. c	14. b	19. e
5. b	10. a	15. d	

True/False Practice Questions

1. According to the Original Study, the Mekranoti had to work hard to get enough produce from their gardens.

2. The Gururumba live in a tropical environment in central Africa.

3. The Bakhtiari are pastoralist nomads who drive their herds throughout the Iran-Iraq border area.

4. Many Bakhtiari are well-educated, having attended university at home or aboard.

5. The spread of malaria was historically linked to the development of slash-and-burn horticulture.

6. In the world today about 3 million people live by food foraging.

7. People started shifting to food-producing ways of life about ten thousand years ago.

8. The average work week of the Ju/'hoansi is about fifty hours.

9. An anthropologist would probably find it difficult to define what "progress" is.

10. The Mekranoti style of slash-and-burn farming did not grow well because animals and insects were constantly invading their gardens.

11. Due to their reliance of slash-and-burn farming the Mekranoti need to work very hard to survive.

12. The Mekranoti constantly weed their gardens to keep the forest from invading.

13. Slash-and-burn agriculture, especially in the humid tropics, may be one of the best gardening techniques possible.

14. Anthropologists were the last to note the possibly disastrous consequences of U.S.-style agriculture in the tropics.

15. According agriculturalists, open-field agriculture is less of a problem than slash-and-burn agriculture.

16. The high fertility of Mekranoti garden plots comes from the soil, not from the trees that are burned there.

17. Because of foraging animals and destructive insects, the Mekranoti could not depend on harvesting whatever they planted.

18. The Mekranoti, it was found, don't have to work very hard to survive.

Answer to true/false practice questions

1. F	6. F	11. F	16. F
2. F	7. T	12. F	17. F
3. T	8. F	13. T	18. T
4. T	9. T	14. F	
5. T	10. F	15. F	

Practice Matching

1. _____ Tsembaga

2. _____ Bakhtiari

3. _____ Comanche

4. _____ Gururumba

5. _____ Aymara

a. Highland Peruvian agriculturalists

b. West Asian pastoralists

c. Horse people of the Great Plains

d. Pig sacrificers of New Guinea

e. Horticulturalists of New Guinea

Answers to practice matching

1. d   2. b   3. c   4. e   5. a

Practice Essays

1. How does Ju/'hoansi social organization relate to the subsistence pattern of hunting and collecting? How is Ju/'hoansi society likely to change as the foraging way of life erodes?

2. Think about your neighborhood. Could it be described as a kind of cultural area, i.e., a geographic region in which a number of different societies follow similar patterns of life? What criteria would be important for defining it that way?

3. The Mekranoti Kayapo employ what has come to be known as slash-and-burn agriculture. Describe the benefits of this style of farming in the tropics. What would be the consequences of a U.S.-style of agriculture in the tropics?

4. As described in your textbook, anthropologist Alan Kolata reintroduced an ancient technology that has improved the lives of the people in an Andean country. Identify the ancient technology and explain why it was lost. Why was it reintroduced? What impact is it having on the quality of life of the people of the area where it was reintroduced?

5. Explain how the anthropologist was able to calculate the productivity of Mekranoti gardens.

Chapter 18
Economic Systems

Synopsis

Chapter 18 discusses the attempt to apply economic theory to non-Western cultures and summarizes the concepts anthropologists have developed to compare the organization of productive resources across cultures. Three major ways of distributing goods and services are described. The relevance of anthropological understanding to international business is also considered.

What you should learn from this chapter

1. Understand how anthropologists use theory to study economic systems.
2. Know the patterns of labor in nonindustrial societies:
   - sexual division of labor
   - division of labor by age
   - cooperation
   - craft specialization
   - control of land
   - technology
3. Understand the methods of distribution and exchange in nonindustrial societies:
   - reciprocity
   - redistribution
   - market exchange

Key Terms and Names

technology

leveling mechanism

reciprocity

generalized reciprocity

balanced reciprocity

negative reciprocity

silent trade

redistribution

Kula ring

Big Man

conspicuous consumption

market exchange

money

informal economy

Review Questions

1. Why might it be misleading to apply contemporary economic theories to preindustrial non-Western societies?

2. Explain the importance of yam production among the Trobrianders.

3. Provide examples that refute the notion of a biological division of labor.

4. Compare and contrast the three general patterns of the sexual division of labor.

5. What are the benefits of the division of labor?

6. How is land controlled in most preindustrial societies?

7. Differentiate between the use of tools in foraging, horticultural, and agricultural communities.

8. Distinguish between industrial and nonindustrial societies with regard to craft specialization.

9. How do societies cooperate in the acquisition of food?

10. Provide some examples of leveling mechanisms.

11. Distinguish between market exchange and marketplace.

12. What are three systems of exchange?

13. What purpose does reciprocity serve?

14. Differentiate between general, balanced, and negative reciprocity.

15. How is trade between groups generally conducted?

16. As discussed in your textbook, describe the relationships between the Kota, Toda, Badaga, and Kurumba of India.

17. What functions does the Kula ring serve?

18. Compare "money" among the Aztec and the Tiv.

19. Why is redistribution generally undertaken?

20. Describe the "informal economy" of North America.

21. How is conspicuous consumption used?

22. Discuss the relevance of anthropology to international business.

23. What are the drawbacks of ethnocentric interpretations of other societies' economic systems?

24. Discuss the role that culture plays in defining the "wants and needs" of a people.

Fill-in-the-Blank

1. All societies have rules pertaining to three productive resources: _____, _____, and _____.

2. Division of labor by sex varies from very flexible to very rigid. Among foragers like the _____, either sex may do the work of the other without loss of face.

3. Rigid division of labor by sex typically occurs with two patterns of subsistence: _____ and _____.

4. In most societies the basic unit in which cooperation takes place is the _____.

5. Among horticulturalists, tools that are typically used are the _____.

6. A _____ works to spread wealth around so that no one accumulates substantially more wealth than anyone else.

7. The economist _____ developed the threefold classification system of reciprocity, redistribution, and market exchange.

8. Types of reciprocity are _____, _____, and _____.

9. The taxation systems of Canada and the United States are examples of _____.

10. In some societies the surplus is used as a display for purposes of prestige. Thorsten Veblen called this _____.

11. Among the Enga of Papua New Guinea, the group that pools its wealth is the _____.

12. The Kota, Toda, Badaga, and Kurumba are interrelated societies in _____.

Exercises

I. When Bronislaw Malinowski studied the Kula ring of the Trobriand Islanders in his classic *Argonauts of the Western Pacific,* he also described other methods of distributing goods in that society as well. Consider each of the following examples of Trobriand exchanges given by Malinowski, and identify whether they can be characterized as forms of reciprocity, redistribution, or market exchange. Then note the elements of each of these forms of exchange in modern North American society as well.

A. *Wasi:* permanent partnerships inland yam-producers inherit with fishermen. When a fisherman brings in a good catch, he takes some fish to his inland partner and gives them as a gift; when the farmer brings in his yam harvest, he takes some to the fisherman as a gift. Neither has any choice about changing partners, neither can bargain for more products, and there is no stated expectation of a return.

B. *Urigubu:* the yam gift that a man gives to his sister's husband every year; it is part of a person's kinship obligations.

C. *Kula:* the exchange between contractual partners of ceremonial/prestige/treasure items.

D. *Pokala:* tribute to a higher-status person, usually a chief.

E. *Sagali:* giveaway feast by a high-status person, usually a chief.

F. *Gim walli:* the moneyless exchange of mundane goods (barter) that occurs after the Kula gift-giving; this exchange occurs between anyone (no contractual partners), and the value seems to be established according to supply and demand and done with a desire to gain the greatest profit.

II. Briefly identify the following cultures, and indicate their locations on the map.

1. Enga

2. Inca

3. Afar

4. Tiv

5. Kota, Toda, Bagada, Kurumba

Multiple-Choice Practice Questions

1. When a man works hard in his horticultural garden in the Trobriand Islands to produce yams, he does this to satisfy which of the following demands?
   a. to have food for his household to eat
   b. to gain prestige by giving yams away to his sisters' husbands
   c. to prove to his wife that he can work as hard as she can
   d. to give the yams to his wife so that she can trade them for goods that they don't produce themselves
   e. to trade for fish

2. The productive resources used by all societies to produce goods and services include
   a. raw materials.
   b. labor.
   c. technology.
   d. bureaucrats.
   e. All but *d*

3. American society's traditional sexual division of labor falls into which pattern?
   a. flexible
   b. rigid segregation
   c. segregation with equality
   d. integrated
   e. cooperative

4. Among the Ju/'hoansi
   a. children are expected to contribute to subsistence from the time they are seven or eight.
   b. elderly people past the age of sixty are expected to contribute hunted or gathered food to the group.
   c. elderly people are a valuable source of knowledge and wisdom about hunting and gathering.
   d. elderly people are taken care of grudgingly because after the age of sixty they contribute nothing to the group.
   e. children are expected to set up their own separate households by the time they are twelve.

5. In many nonindustrial societies,
   a. people prefer to have fun rather than to work.
   b. cooperative work is usually done with a festive, sociable air.
   c. cooperative work is always done in the household.
   d. cooperative work groups are organized primarily for profit.
   e. solitary work is preferred to cooperative work.

6. Among food foragers such as the Ju/'hoansi,
   a. land is defined as a territory with usable resources and flexible boundaries that belongs to a band that has occupied it for a long time.
   b. land is thought of as belonging to those who have bought it.
   c. land is considered private property, and access to the land can be denied.
   d. land has clear-cut boundaries marked by survey posts.
   e. land is controlled by a corporation of strangers.

7. In nonindustrial societies, when a tool is complex and difficult to make it is usually considered to be owned by
   a. the whole village in which it is used.
   b. a single individual.
   c. the state.
   d. all those who touch it.
   e. all relatives.

8. Leveling mechanisms
   a. are more common in hunter-gatherer societies than in agricultural communities.
   b. result in one family becoming wealthier than others.
   c. are found in communities where property must not be allowed to threaten an egalitarian social order.
   d. are more common in industrial societies than in agricultural societies.
   e. no longer exist.

9. The mode of distribution called reciprocity refers to the exchange of goods and services
   a. of unequal value.
   b. between persons in hierarchical relationships.
   c. for the purpose of maintaining social relationships and gaining prestige.
   d. to make a profit.
   e. to embarrass the person who gave the least.

10. A Navaho gives ten of his sheep that he knows are infected with disease to a Hopi in exchange for a jeep. This is an example of
    a. generalized reciprocity.
    b. balanced reciprocity.
    c. negative reciprocity.
    d. silent trade.
    e. redistribution.

11. The Kula ring
    a. is a marriage ring made of shells.
    b. is found among the Ju/'hoansi.
    c. is found among the Andaman Islanders.
    d. is a circular trade route along which various goods flow.
    e. is a form of silent trade.

12. The American system of paying income taxes every April is an example of
    a. generalized reciprocity.
    b. balanced reciprocity.
    c. negative reciprocity.
    d. redistribution.
    e. market exchange.

13. The display of wealth for social prestige is called
    a. a leveling mechanism.
    b. conspicuous consumption.
    c. redistribution.
    d. balanced reciprocity.
    e. barter.

14. Formal market exchange is usually associated with
    a. hunting and gathering bands.
    b. horticultural tribes.
    c. pastoral tribes.
    d. a state type of political organization.
    e. the household as the unit of production and consumption.

15. A businessperson who wants to build a factory in the Middle East could benefit from the contributions of a cultural anthropologist. In which of the following ways would an anthropologist be likely to help?
    a. provide knowledge of the principles of market exchange
    b. introduce a new method of paying local workers
    c. tell the businessperson how to sit, dress, and talk when making the arrangements with local people.
    d. screen workers who have diseases
    e. *b* and *c*

16. An example of tribal leadership is the _____. Such men are leaders of a localized descent group or of a territorial group.
   a. manager
   b. Big Man
   c. mayor
   d. shaman
   e. chairman

17. The group discussed in the article, *Prestige Economics in Papua New Guinea,* was the _____.
   a. Kaluli
   b. Kapauku
   c. Enga
   d. Mekranoti
   e. Mende

18. Not only have anthropologists found niches for themselves in the world of business, but since 1972, the number of them going into business has grown _____.
   a. tenfold
   b. fivefold
   c. 50%
   d. anthropologists don't work in the business world
   e. 25%

19. One of the newest innovations in the market-research and design industry is _____.
   a. survey questionnaire
   b. telephone surveys
   c. ethnology
   d. ethnography
   e. case studies

Answers to multiple-choice practice questions

1. b	6. a	11. d	16. b
2. e	7. b	12. d	17. c
3. b	8. c	13. b	18. b
4. c	9. c	14. d	19. d
5. b	10. c	15. e	

True/False Practice Questions

1. According to Robert Lowie, patterns of reciprocity among the Crow did not involve women.

2. In "silent trade," no words are spoken, but the participants must meet face to face to exchange goods.

3. The Inca empire of Peru featured a highly efficient redistributive system.

4. The economist responsible for the concept of "conspicuous consumption" was Thorsten Veblen.

5. The Enga live in Indonesia.

6. Jomo Kenyatta was an anthropologist who became "the father" of modern Kenya.

7. The Big Man feasts exist merely as arenas for grandiose men to flaunt their ambition.

8. Big Man feasts are like conspicuous consumption in Western societies; the emphasis is on the hoarding of goods that would make them unavailable to others.

9. Anthropologists only work in exotic, faraway places like remote islands, deep forests, hostile deserts, or arctic wastelands.

10. There is a potential job market for anthropologists in the market-research and design area.

11. According to your textbook, most anthropologists who work at market-research and design companies are not really "doing ethnography."

Answers to true/false practice questions

1. F	5. F	9. F
2. F	6. T	10. T
3. T	7. F	11. T
4. T	8. F	

Practice Essays

1. Compare and contrast the different ideas about the nature and control of land that exist among food foragers, horticulturalists, pastoralists, intensive agriculturalists, and industrialists.

2. Compare and contrast the different ideas about tools and tool ownership in foraging, horticultural, and intensive agricultural societies.

3. Describe the ecological context of the "Big Man" system of the Enga.

4. Describe the prestige economies of the Enga. Explain their function and purpose.

5. Describe what an anthropologist can contribute to the world of business.

Chapter 19
Sex and Marriage

Synopsis

Chapter 19 defines marriage as a system for regulating sexual access and explores the variations on the theme of marriage throughout the world. The interactions of marriage, social structure, and environment are considered.

What you should learn from this chapter

1. Understand what marriage is in nonethnocentric terms.
2. Know the controls societies place on sexual relations and theories as to why these controls are necessary.
3. Understand the many forms of marriage and how they relate with other aspects of society:
   - monogamy
   - polygyny
   - polyandry
   - two forms of cousin marriage
4. Understand the role of consanguineal and affinal ties in society.
5. Know the kinds of gift exchanges that often accompany marriage.

Key Terms and Names

marriage

Claude Levi-Strauss

affinal kin

conjugal bond

consanguineal kin

incest taboo

endogamy

exogamy

monogamy

family

consanguine family

nuclear family

polygyny

polyandry

group marriage

levirate

sororate

serial monogamy

patrilateral parallel-cousin marriage

matrilateral cross-cousin marriage

bride price

bride service

dowry

Review Questions

1. Why are human females able to engage in sexual activity regardless of their ovulation cycles?

2. Why does sexual activity require social control?

3. Describe the sex life of the Trobrianders.

4. As discussed in your textbook, describe the traditional marriage system of the Nayar.

5. What is the incest taboo?

6. Why do people who live in close proximity to one another exhibit reduced sexual activity?

7. What are the Oedipus and Electra complexes?

8. How have geneticists attempted to explain the incest taboo?

9. Distinguish between endogamy and exogamy.

10. What were the initial reasons for exogamy, according to Tylor, Levi-Strauss, and Cohen?

11. Distinguish between marriage and mating.

12. To what extent can North American society be characterized as monogamous?

13. Provide a nonethnocentric definition of marriage.

14. Distinguish between consanguineal and conjugal families.

15. Distinguish between polygynous and polyandrous families.

16. What form of marriage does the majority of the world's societies exhibit?

17. Characterize the typical polygynous society.

18. What is the attitude of Kapauku women towards their husbands' other wives?

19. Describe the social and economic context of polyandry.

20. Discuss the contexts in which sororate, levirate, and serial monogamy are likely to occur.

21. What benefits do arranged marriages have?

22. Describe the marriage system of Sidi Embarek, Morocco.

23. Distinguish between patrilineal parallel-cousin and matrilineal cross-cousin marriage.

24. How is marriage exchange conducted among the Trobrianders?

25. Distinguish between bride price, dowry, and bride service.

26. What is the function of female-female marriage among the Nandi?

27. What role can anthropologists play in the study of AIDS?

Fill-in-the-Blank

1. Marriage is a cultural transaction that regulates men's and women's rights of _____ access to one another and defines the context in which women are eligible to bear children.

2. The female ability to engage is sexual relations at any time is related to the development of _____ locomotion among the hominines.

3. Only about _____ percent of the world's societies prohibit all sexual involvement outside of marriage.

4. The bond between two individuals joined by marriage is called a(n) _____ bond.

5. Households composed only of "'blood" relatives are said to contain _____ kin.

6. The _____ taboo prohibits sexual relations between specified individuals.

7. _____ is a rule mandating the one marry outside of a particular group, while _____ mandates marriage within the group.

8. In the United States, _____ is the only legally recognized form of marriage, but some Americans do engage in other forms.

9. A _____ family contains a husband and his multiple wives, while a _____ family contains a wife and her multiple husbands.

10. Among the Turkana of northern Kenya, _____ is the preferred form of marriage.

11. When the wives in a polygynous marriage are sisters, this is called _____ polygyny.

12. _____ marriage refers to a marriage in which several men and women have sexual access to one another.

13. In a _____, a widow marries the brother of her deceased husband; in a _____, a widower marries the sister of his deceased wife.

14. Marrying a sequence of partners throughout one's life is called _____.

15. In a patrilateral parallel-cousin marriage, a boy marries his father's _____ daughter.

16. _____ is a gift exchange occurring at marriage in which money or goods are transferred from the groom's side to the bride's.

17. In a _____ system, the bride's family provides money or goods at the time of marriage.

18. The Nandi of western Kenya practice a form of marriage in which a woman marries _____.

19. Divorce rates in Western society are considered high by many people but are low compared to divorce rates among _____ societies.

20. _____ is a French anthropologist who launched a school of thought called structuralism.

21. Medical anthropologists can contribute significantly to the study of _____ through investigating the social and sexual contexts of disease transmission in various societies.

Exercises

I. Draw your family tree in the place below. Make it as extensive as you can without consulting any of your relatives. What accounts for the relatively truncated kindreds of most North Americans?

II. Briefly identify and locate the following cultures on the map.

1. Nayar   2. Nandi

3. Morocco   4. Tibet

Multiple-Choice Practice Questions

1. _____ is a transaction in which a woman and man establish a continuing claim to the right of sexual access to one another, and in which the woman involved becomes eligible to bear children.
   a. Family
   b. Marriage
   c. Incest
   d. Affinity
   e. Sex

2. One explanation for the tendency of human females to be sexually receptive on a continuing basis is that
   a. it is an accidental byproduct of the high hormone requirements for persistent bipedal locomotion.
   b. it increases competitiveness among the males of a group.
   c. it encourages endogamy.
   d. it discourages incest.
   e. it leads to greater competitiveness among women.

3. Marriage resolves the problem of how to bring sexual activity under _____ control.
   a. biological
   b. male
   c. cultural
   d. female
   e. mother-in-law

4. A household composed of married people contains _____ kin.
   a. affinal
   b. consanguineal
   c. endogamous
   d. nuclear
   e. instinctive

5. According to the _____ theory of incest taboo, children feel so guilty about their sexual feelings for a parent that they repress them, and this is expressed culturally in the incest taboo.
   a. genetic
   b. instinctive
   c. psychological
   d. anthropological
   e. sociological

6. Although all societies have some kind of incest taboo, the relationship that is considered incestuous may vary. Concepts of incest seem to be related to a group's definitions of endogamy and exogamy, thus suggesting that incest taboos may help to promote
   a. alliances between groups.
   b. inbreeding.
   c. brother-sister marriages.
   d. parallel-cousin marriages.
   e. cross-cousin marriages.

7. Marriage within a particular group of individuals is called
   a. incest.
   b. exogamy.
   c. monogamy.
   d. endogamy.
   e. polygamy.

8. The French anthropologist Claude Levi-Strauss says that the incest taboo is universal because humans
   a. are instinctively opposed to inbreeding.
   b. repress their sexual desire for the parent of the opposite sex.
   c. have learned to establish alliances with strangers and thereby share and develop culture.
   d. prefer to marry their brothers and sisters.
   e. don't like sex.

9. A residential kin group composed of a woman, her dependent children, and at least one adult male joined through marriage or blood relationship is a/an
   a. family.
   b. conjugal bond.
   c. endogamous.
   d. nuclear family.
   e. serial marriage.

10. Families can be consanguineal or conjugal. The conjugal family has many forms. One type of conjugal family is the _____, consisting of the husband, wife, and dependent children.
    a. polygynous family
    b. polygamous family
    c. polyandrous family
    d. nuclear family
    e. extended family

11. Although _____ may statistically be the most common form of marriage around the world, it is not the most preferred.
    a. polygyny
    b. monogamy
    c. polyandry
    d. polygamy
    e. the levirate

12. Polygyny
    a. means marriage to more than one man.
    b. is the most common form of marriage.
    c. is usually possible only when a man is fairly wealthy.
    d. is less common than polyandry.
    e. is an example of group marriage.

13. An example of group marriage would be
    a. a pastoral nomad's wife among the Turkana who actively searches for another woman to share her husband and her work with the livestock.
    b. the Moonies having a large wedding ceremony at which five hundred couples, each one assigned to another, are married at the same time.
    c. a prosperous member of the Kapauku in western New Guinea who is able to afford a bride price for four wives.
    d. a hippy commune in the Haight-Ashbury district in which it is accepted that all adult members of the commune have sexual access to each other.
    e. a Nayar household in which a woman takes several lovers.

14. The levirate and the sororate
    a. are secret societies, like sororities and fraternities.
    b. function to maintain the relationship between the family of the bride and the family of the groom.
    c. are *usually* possible only when the man is fairly wealthy.
    d. are types of cattle in pastoralist societies.
    e. exist only in advanced industrial societies.

15. Serial monogamy tends to occur in societies where
    a. a woman with children receives a great deal of help from her mother and brothers.
    b. women do not have many children.
    c. a woman with dependent children, isolated from her parents, marries a series of partners to get the assistance of another adult.
    d. women are very wealthy.
    e. divorce is forbidden.

16. The main function of a bride price is
    a. for a man to show off to his wife how rich he is.
    b. for a man to buy a slave.
    c. for the wife's people to gain prestige in the village.
    d. to compensate the wife's family for her labor.
    e. for the wife's people to buy a husband for their daughter.

17. When a man marries his father's brother's daughter in ancient Greece or traditional China,
    a. he is committing incest.
    b. he is practicing matrilineal cross-cousin marriage.
    c. he is practicing patrilateral cross-cousin marriage.
    d. he is keeping property within the single male line of descent.
    e. *c* and *d*

18. In which of the following situations would you expect to find the custom of bride price?
    a. A bride and groom leave the community after marriage and set up their own household in a distant city.
    b. A bride and groom go to live with the bride's people.
    c. A bride and groom go to live with the groom's people.
    d. A bride and groom go to live with the bride's mother's brother.
    e. None of the above

19. When the economy is based on _____ and where the man does most of the productive work, the bride's people may give a dowry that protects the woman against desertion and is a statement of her economic status.
    a. food foraging
    b. pastoralism
    c. intensive agriculture
    d. horticulture
    e. industrialism

20. The woman/woman marriage custom found in sub-Saharan Africa
    a. enables a woman without sons to inherit a share of her husband's property.
    b. confers legitimacy on the children of a woman who had been unable to find a husband.
    c. enables the woman who adopts a male identity to raise her status.
    d. enables the woman who is the wife of the female husband to raise her status and live a more secure life.
    e. All of the above

21. Which of the following constitutes a culturally valid reason for divorce among different groups?
    a. sterility or impotence
    b. cruelty
    c. being a poor provider
    d. being a lazy housekeeper
    e. All of the above

22. In an arranged marriage in India, the newly married couple will go to live in a _____ family.
    a. nuclear
    b. combined
    c. mixed
    d. joint
    e. consanguine

23. According to the article in your textbook '"Arranging Marriage in India," among urban Indians an important source of contacts in trying to arrange a marriage is/are the _____.
    a. social club.
    b. newspaper personals.
    c. internet chat rooms.
    d. match making businesses.
    e. temple.

24. Which of the following characteristics would be most important in an Indian family's selection of a bride for their son?
    a. good looks
    b. well-educated
    c. independent
    d. have higher social status
    e. good character

25. _____ is the leading exponent of French structuralism.
    a. Bronislaw Malinowski
    b. Franz Boas
    c. Claude Levi-Strauss
    d. Phillipe Cousteau
    e. Emile Durkiem

Answers to multiple-choice practice questions

1. b	8. c	15. c	22. d
2. a	9. a	16. d	23. a
3. c	10. d	17. e	24. e
4. a	11. b	18. c	25. c
5. c	12. c	19. c	
6. a	13. d	20. e	
7. d	14. b	21. e	

True/False Practice Questions

1. Trobriand children begin sexual experimentation at a young age.

2. About half of the world's societies prohibit sexual involvement outside of marriage.

3. Haviland believes that evidence on intrafamily homicides support Freud's theories of the Oedipus and Electra complex.

4. Brother-sister marriages were common among farmers in Roman Egypt.

5. Primate evidence shows that it is likely that humans started out as a monogamous species.

6. People want pretty much the same things in marriage whether it is in India or America.

7. Today, a dowry is expected by law in India.

8. In India it is understood that matches (marriages) would be arranged only within the same caste and general social class.

9. In India no crossing of subcastes is permissible even if the class positions of the bride's and groom's families are similar.

10. As far as arranging a marriage is concerned, in India the basic rule seems to be that a family's reputation is most important.

11. Although it is common for the newly married Indian couple to go live with the groom's joint family in the rural area, it is not common among the urban, upper-middle class in India.

12. In India divorce is still a scandal and thus the divorce rate is exceedingly low.

13. When arranging an Indian marriage, consideration of a girl's looks are more important than her character.

14. In an arranged marriage in India, a woman is being judged as a prospective daughter-in-law as much as a prospective bride.

15. In an arranged Indian marriage, offering the proper gifts is often an important factor in influencing the relationship between the bride's and groom's families, and the treatment of the bride in her new home.

16. In India a military career with its economic security has great prestige and is considered a benefit in finding a suitable bride.

17. While a boy's skin color is a less important consideration than a girl's, it is still a factor when arranging a marriage in India.

Answers to true/false practice questions

1. T	7. F	13. F
2. F	8. T	14. T
3. F	9. F	15. T
4. T	10. T	16. T
5. F	11. F	17. T
6. F	12. T	

Practice Matching

Match the culture with its characteristic.

1. _____ Nandi

2. _____ Moroccans

3. _____ Nayar

4. _____ Tibetans

5. _____ North Americans

a. A culture emphasizing love and choice as a basis for marriage

b. South Indian people who give the mother's brothers key responsibility in child rearing

c. Patrilineal North African people who practice arranged marriage

d. East African pastoralists who practice woman/woman marriage

e. Polyandrous society of central Asia

Answers to practice matching

1. d   2. c   3. b   4. e   5. a

Practice Essays

1. Describe how the "romantic love" complex impacts North American marriage patterns. Is romantic love involved in marriage in India? Discuss why or why not?

2. What factors affect the stability of marriages and the choice of mates?

3. What factors must be taken into consideration when arranging a marriage in India? Describe.

4. Describe the contributions of anthropologists to our understanding and control of AIDS.

Chapter 20
Family and Household

Synopsis

Chapter 20 focuses on the differences between families and households, noting that the Western assumption that all households are built around conjugal relationships is ethnocentric. The major residence patterns are defined, and the various problems created by different kinds of living arrangements are explored.

What you should learn from this chapter

1. Understand the functions of the family in human society and the difference between family and household.
2. Know the various forms of family organization and the difficulties associated with each:
   - polygynous
   - extended
   - nuclear
   - female-headed
3. Know the basic kinds of residence rules that are found in diverse societies:
   - patrilocal
   - matrilocal
   - ambilocal
   - neolocal
   - avunculocal

Key Terms

household

conjugal family

268 CHAPTER 20 Family and Household

extended family

patrilocal residence

matrilocal residence

ambilocal residence

neolocal residence

avunculocal residence

Review Questions

1. How does Haviland define "family?"

2. How did historical and social circumstances shape the character of the Western family?

3. Describe the care and nurturance of the young among primates.

4. Describe the various ways in which households can be structured.

5. How is the modern American family related to the rise of industrial capitalism?

6. Describe the nuclear family.

7. What relations might be a part of the extended family?

8. What societal factors might contribute to the existence of extended families?

9. Distinguish the five common patterns of residence.

10. How does ecology impact residence pattern?

11. What residence pattern was traditionally followed by people along the Maine coast and why?

12. What residence pattern was traditionally followed by the Hopi and how did it influence family life?

13. What problems may accompany polygynous families and how are they handled?

14. What problems may accompany extended families and how are they resolved?

15. What problems may accompany nuclear families and how are they worked out?

16. What problems may accompany female-headed families and how are they dealt with?

17. How was Dr. Margaret Boone able to impact policies relating to infant mortality in Washington, D.C.?

18. How does the status of women relate to various kinds of family and residence patterns?

Fill-in-the-Blank

1. The independent nuclear family emerged in Europe in the fourth century A.D. in response regulations put forward by _____.

2. The "ephemeral modern family" that developed in conjunction with industrial capitalism was studied by _____.

3. A family based on a marital tie is called a _____ family, while a family based on blood ties is called a _____ family.

4. A _____ is a residential group composed of a woman, her dependent children, and at least one male joined through marriage or a blood relationship.

5. Among the Mundurucu, after age thirteen boys go to live in _____.

6. Two examples of the rare consanguineal family are the _____ and the _____.

7. Two examples of societies based on independent nuclear families are the _____ and the _____.

8. In a _____ form of residence, husbands go to live with their wife's parents after marriage.

9. In a _____ form of residence, wives go to live with their husband's parents after marriage.

10. The Hopi practice _____ residence while the Chinese practice _____ residence.

11. Among the Trobrianders, a newly married couple goes to live with the groom's mother's brother. This is called _____ residence.

12. The Mbuti practice _____ residence.

13. Dr. Margaret Boone studied the problem of _____ in Washington, D.C.

Exercises

I. Anthropologists have developed a method of expressing kin relationships symbolically. In this form of notation, males are represented by triangles and females by circles. A bond of marriage is represented by an equal sign (two parallel lines) while a consanguineal bond is represented by a single line. For example, the following diagram shows a conventional nuclear family of a husband, wife, and two children:

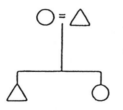

There are further specifications possible in the standard genealogical notation. If an individual is deceased, he or she is represented by a diagonal line drawn through the triangle or circle. Here is a diagram of a widow with her three sons and one daughter. In the society in which this hypothetical family lives, goods are inherited through the female line, from mother to daughter. This is indicated on the diagram by coloring in the triangles and circles in the line of inheritance (the lineage).

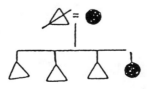

Sometimes other kinds of modifications can be added to a genealogical chart as well. For example, a residence group might be indicated by drawing a line around the individuals included in the household. For example, the following shows an extended family household based on ties between brothers.

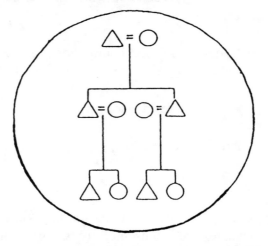

Now redraw your family tree from Chapter 8 using standard genealogical notation. (Don't worry about inheritance or residence here; just diagram the basic affinal and consanguineal ties).

II. On the three charts below, illustrate a *patrilocal* residence group, a *matrilocal* residence group, and an *avunculocal* residence group by drawing a line around the included individuals.

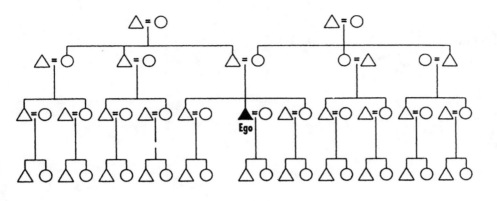

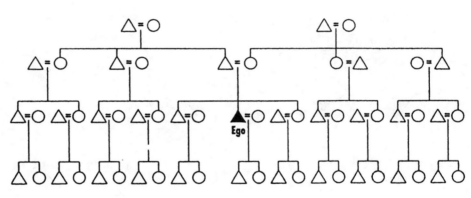

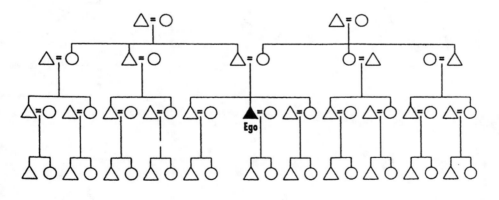

III. Briefly identify and locate the following cultures:

    1. Mundurucu   2. Tory Islanders

    3. Coastal Mainers   4. Inuit

    5. Hopi

Multiple-Choice Practice Questions

1. The independent nuclear family in Europe
   a. emerged recently as the result of regulations passed by the Roman Catholic Church in the fourth century A.D.
   b. is a universal family form that is natural to primates.
   c. is found only in Europe and places to which Europeans have emigrated.
   d. is found only in non-Western societies.
   e. was the only form of family considered legitimate in the Old Testament of the Bible.

2. The effect of industrialization on nuclear families was
   a. an increased dependence on extended kin, who could provide aid during difficult times.
   b. greater isolation because of the mobility required of an industrial labor force.
   c. greater conflict among members of the nuclear family over scarce jobs.
   d. the tendency to develop polygyny.
   e. the tendency to develop the levirate.

3. Which of the following statements is CORRECT?
   a. The period of infant dependency in humans is the same as that in other primates.
   b. The family is the only unit in which children can be reared in a nurturant manner.
   c. Only among humans are males larger and stronger than females.
   d. Human infants can survive only with the care provided by the biological mother.
   e. None of the above

4. A household is
   a. a residential group composed of a woman, her dependent children, and at least one male joined through marriage or consanguineal relationship.
   b. a nonresidential group composed of people who share common interests.
   c. a residential unit within which economic production, consumption, inheritance, child rearing and shelter are organized and carried out.
   d. a temporary association of strangers.
   e. a research center.

5. A residential kin group composed of related women, their brothers, and the women's offspring is
   a. a conjugal family.
   b. an extended family.
   c. a consanguineal family.
   d. a nuclear family.
   e. a patrilocal family.

6. What do traditional Inuit society and contemporary North American society have in common that explains the similarity in their family structure?
   a. Both developed in arctic environments.
   b. Both rely on the technology of hunting.
   c. In both, people have very few possessions so there is little jealousy.
   d. Both care for their elderly.
   e. Both are highly mobile.

7. The _____ is composed of people related to each other by ties of blood who bring their spouses to live in the family.
   a. extended family
   b. polygamous family
   c. consanguine family
   d. nuclear family
   e. communal family

8. Residence patterns refer to
   a. how a group makes its living in a particular environment.
   b. the structure of a family under certain ecological conditions.
   c. where a couple chooses to live after they are married.
   d. the problems that different families have.
   e. whether the husband and wife sleep in the same room or in different rooms after they are married.

9. Societies that rely on animal husbandry or intensive agriculture, in which polygyny is customary and where warfare is prominent enough to make male cooperation important, are most likely to practice _____ residence.
   a. matrilocal
   b. avunculocal
   c. ambilocal
   d. patrilocal
   e. neolocal

10. Ambilocal residence is found in societies
   a. that stress the cooperation of women.
   b. where warfare is common and men wield authority.
   c. where economic activity occurs outside the family, and families have to move frequently in search of jobs.
   d. where males control property but descent and inheritance are reckoned through women.
   e. where the nuclear family is not sufficient to handle the economic activities required for the family's survival, but resources are limited.

11. Neolocal residence is common in industrial societies like our own because
    a. newlyweds do not usually get along with their in-laws.
    b. industries require workers to be able to move to wherever there are jobs.
    c. most families set up their own businesses, and they do not require the labor of other family members outside the nuclear family.
    d. brothers need to stay together for purposes of conducting warfare.
    e. women continue to live with their brothers after marriage.

12. Which of the following statements about residence patterns in the Trobriand Islands is INCORRECT?
    a. All couples live with the husband's mother's brother.
    b. Men who are in line to take over control of their descent group's assets will take their wives to live with their mother's brother.
    c. Most couples live patrilocally.
    d. Men who live with their fathers gain access to land controlled by their fathers' descent groups.
    e. Men who live with their fathers also have access to land controlled through female descent.

13. A man who marries several sisters is practicing
    a. avunculocal residence.
    b. sororal polygyny.
    c. fraternal polyandry.
    d. infidelity.
    e. matrilocal residence.

14. Extended families usually work more effectively if authority is in the hands of one person, such as the eldest son. Which of the following methods of reducing conflict between this eldest son and his younger brothers are likely to be found in extended families?
    a. moving out of the household
    b. dependence training
    c. independence training
    d. increasing the number of wives for the younger sons
    e. murder of the eldest son

15. Extended families have which of the following problems?
    a. loneliness caused by isolation from kin
    b. children are raised to be independent, which competes with group harmony
    c. the eldest son is in competition with his younger brothers for the position of authority in the household
    d. mothers-in-law are powerless
    e. mother's brother is the authority figure

16. What are some of the problems associated with the nuclear family?
    a. Husbands and wives tend to be isolated from their kin.
    b. There are no clear-cut lines of authority and rules for making decisions.
    c. The elderly cannot depend on their children for aid when they are too old to take care of themselves.
    d. There is very little privacy.
    e. All but *d*

17. The increase in number of single-parent households headed by women is likely to be associated with
    a. increased child support being paid by fathers.
    b. increased participation of extended kin in caring for the children.
    c. increased number of women below the poverty line.
    d. decreased number of welfare programs.
    e. decreased number of women below the poverty line in third-world countries.

18. In 1979 anthropologist _____set about to gain an understanding of the sociocultural basis of poor maternal and infant health among inner city African Americans.
    a. Margaret Mead
    b. Margaret Boone
    c. Barbara Myerhoff
    d. Alan Kolata
    e. Fred Plog

19. Which of the following were found to be contributing factors to infant death and miscarriage among African-American women in the Washington, D.C. study?
    a. smoking
    b. absence of prenatal care
    c. alcohol consumption
    d. rapid childbearing in the teens
    e. All of the above are contributing factors

20. Single parent households headed by women have been known and studied for a long time in the _____.
    a. countries of southern Europe.
    b. country of India.
    c. countries of Central America.
    d. countries of the Caribbean basin.
    e. countries of sub-Saharan Africa.

Answers to multiple-choice practice questions

1. a	6. e	11. b	16. e
2. b	7. a	12. a	17. c
3. e	8. c	13. b	18. b
4. c	9. d	14. b	19. e
5. c	10. e	15. c	20. d

True/False Practice Questions

1. A woman who marries several brothers is practicing sororal polygyny.

2. Neolocal residence is common when the nuclear family must be able to move independently.

3. Among the Mundurucu, the men's houses and the women's houses constitute separate families.

4. Among the Hopi, daughters brought their husbands to live near their mother's house.

5. In an avunculocal residence pattern, the newly married couple goes to live with the bride's father's sister.

6. In Washington D.C., as in the rest of the United States, infant mortality is mainly an African-American health problem.

7. In the U.S. African-American infants die at almost twice the rate of "white" infants.

8. In the Washington D.C. infant mortality study it was found that heroin abuse was a more important factor than alcohol abuse.

9. It is now widely recognized that the problem of infant mortality goes beyond mere medicine, and that medical solutions have gone about as far as they can go.

10. According Boone's study, social and cultural factors are not connected to poor health of inner-city African-Americans.

11. Female-headed households are in fact a pathological response to economic restraints in U.S. society.

12. Single parent households headed by women are relatively rare and are restricted to industrialized societies like the United States.

13. Women constitute the majority of the poor, the underprivileged and the economically and socially disadvantaged in most of the world's societies, just as is becoming the case in the U.S.

Answers to true/false practice questions

1. F	6. T	11. F
2. T	7. T	12. F
3. F	8. F	13. T
4. T	9. T	
5. F	10. F	

Practice Matching

Match the culture with its characteristic.

1. _____ Inuit

2. _____ Coastal Mainers

3. _____ Mundurucu

4. _____ Tory Islanders

5. _____ Hopi

a. Irish society centered on consanguineal families

b. Amazon people with "men's houses"

c. Americans maintaining an extended family tradition

d. Southwestern Native Americans with families headed by women

e. Arctic people who live in nuclear families

Answers to practice matching

1. e   2. c   3. b   4. a   5. d

Practice Essay

1. Senator Daniel Patrick Moynihan was the author of a classic study on the problems of urban black people in the United States. Known as "the Moynihan Report," this document blamed irresponsible males and the resultant female-headed families for many of the ills that plague the African-American community. How might an anthropologist respond to this claim? (In fact, an anthropologist did respond to it. Her name is Carol Stack and her book *All Our Kin* was a significant landmark in our understanding of African-American culture. You might like to have a look at both the Moynihan report and *All Our Kin* to see how anthropological insights can contribute to more appropriate government policies.)

2. Describe Margaret Boone's study on infant mortality in Washington D.C. What methods did she use to gather data? What conclusions did she reach after analyzing her data. What were the implications of her study?

3. Identify and discuss the problems inherent in the "traditional" nuclear family.

Chapter 21
Kinship and Descent

Synopsis

Chapter 21 presents some key concepts relating to the anthropological study of kinship and descent. The relationship of kinship patterns to other elements of social organization is explored.

What You Should Learn From This Chapter

1. Know the difference between kindreds and lineal descent groups.
2. Understand the various types of descent systems:
   - patrilineal
   - matrilineal
   - double descent
   - ambilineal
3. Understand the organization and function of descent groups:
   - lineage
   - clan
   - phratry
   - moiety
4. Recognize the major systems of kinship terminology:
   - Eskimo
   - Hawaiian
   - Iroquois
   - Crow
   - Omaha
   - Descriptive

Key Terms and Names

descent group

Lewis Henry Morgan

unilineal descent

matrilineal descent

patrilineal descent

double descent

ambilineal descent

lineage

fission

clan

totemism

phratry

moiety

kindred

Eskimo system

Hawaiian system

Iroquois system

Crow system

Omaha system

Sudanese or Descriptive system

Review Questions

1. Why do societies form descent groups?

2. How is membership in a descent group restricted?

3. Distinguish between patrilineal and matrilineal descent groups

4. What function does double descent serve in Yako society?

5. Explain the function of ambilineal descent in contemporary North America. Provide an example.

6. What functions do descent groups serve?

7. How is a lineage reckoned?

8. What are the social implications of lineage exogamy?

9. Contrast a clan and a lineage.

10. What did anthropologist M. Wolf find out about the situation of women in Taiwan?

11. What purpose do totems serve a clan?

12. Distinguish between a phratry and a moiety.

13. How do bilateral systems differ from unilateral systems?

14. What are the functions and limitations of ego-centered groups?

15. Why do descent groups emerge?

16. What functions do kinship terminologies serve?

17. What are the six major systems of kinship terminology?

18. What is the main feature of the Eskimo system of descent?

19. What is the simplest descent system? Why is it considered simple?

20. With which type of descent group is Iroquois terminology commonly correlated?

21. How can anthropologists assist Native Americans in their struggles for federal recognition?

Exercises

I. On the two charts provided below, color in a *matrilineal descent group* and a *patrilineal descent group.*

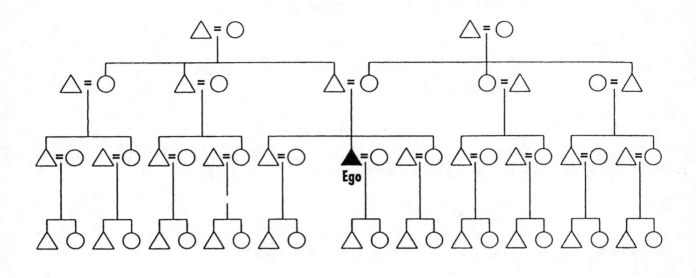

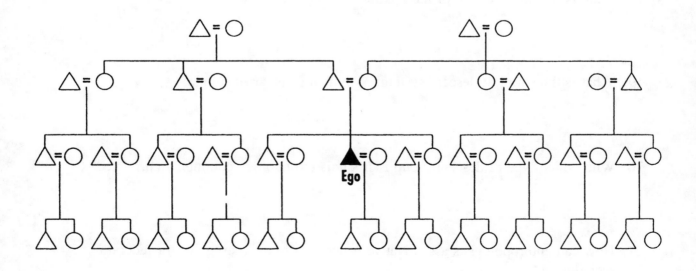

II. What kind of terminological system is shown here?

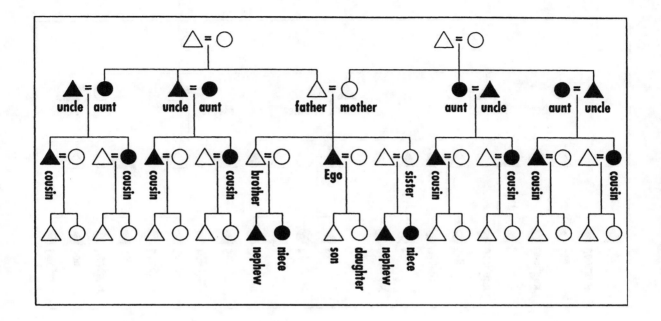

III. What kind of terminological system is shown here?

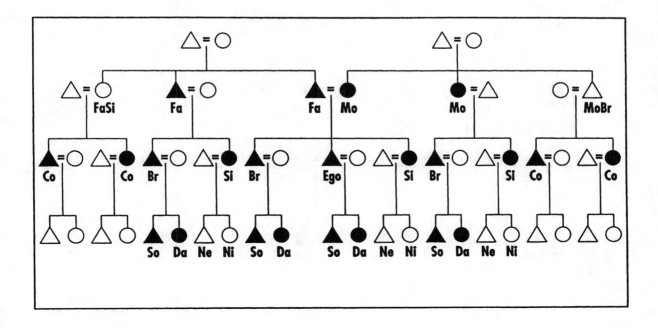

IV. What kind of terminological system is shown here?

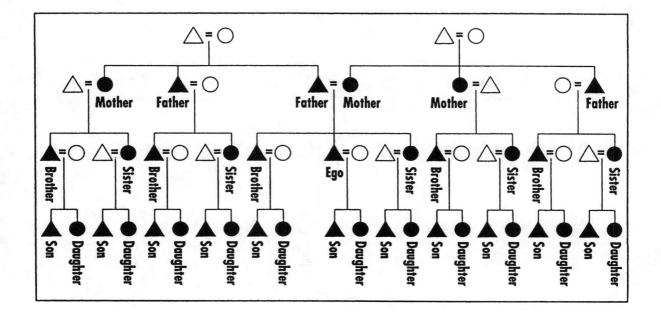

V. In the system below, what should Ego call the individual marked "X"?

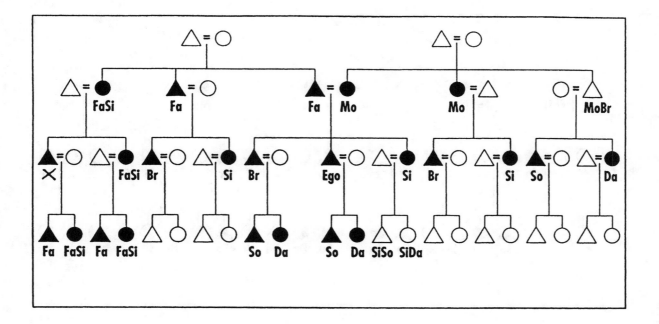

VI. On the chart below, illustrate a descriptive type terminological system.

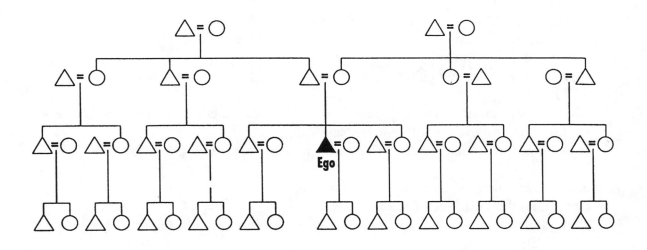

Multiple-Choice Practice Questions

1. Descent groups
   a. are composed of those who claim to be lineally descended from a particular ancestor.
   b. are common in human societies.
   c. trace their connections back to a common ancestor through a chain of parent-child links, and thus appear to stem from the parent-child bond.
   d. help provide jobs for their members.
   e. all but *d*

2. By tracing membership either through males or through females, members of unilineal descent groups
   a. know exactly to which group they belong and where their primary loyalties lie.
   b. are confused about their relationship to persons not included in the group.
   c. act like females if they are in a matrilineal group.
   d. act life males if they are in a patrilineal group.
   e. know exactly how many children they are going to have.

3. You belong to a patrilineal descent group. Which of the following belong to the same group?
    a. your mother
    b. your father's sister
    c. your mother's sister
    d. your mother's father
    e. your father's sister's children

4. The primary way in which a woman in traditional China could exert any influence was
    a. through her close tie with her husband.
    b. by appealing to her mother-in-law who will intercede with her husband on her behalf.
    c. by threatening to return to her own people.
    d. through the influence of her brothers.
    e. through the village women's gossip which can cause a loss of face for her husband and father-in-law.

5. A boy is born into a society that practices matrilineal descent. The person who exercises authority over him is
    a. his sister.
    b. his father.
    c. his mother.
    d. his mother's brother.
    e. his father's sister.

6. Among the Yako of Nigeria, an individual might inherit grazing lands from his father's patrilineal group, and livestock and ritual knowledge from his mother's matrilineal group. This is an example of _____ descent.
    a. ambilineal
    b. bilocal
    c. patrilateral
    d. indivisible
    e. double

7. A cousins club _____
    a. is an ambilineal descent group to which younger-generation descendants of east European Jewish immigrants belong.
    b. is a double descent group to which only cross cousins belong.
    c. is a patrilineal descent group composed of the children of Norman Cousins.
    d. is a cognatic descent group composed of women only.
    e. is a unilineal descent group for first and second cousins.

8. Descent groups
    a. are economic units providing mutual aid.
    b. provide social security for elderly members.
    c. often promote solidarity by encouraging worship of the group's ancestors.
    d. play a role in deciding appropriate marriage partners.
    e. all of the above

9. A lineage is a corporate descent group
    a. the members of which can buy shares in the corporation.
    b. the members of which claim descent from a common ancestor.
    c. the members of which know the exact genealogical linkages by which they are related to the common ancestor.
    d. composed of consanguineal kin.
    e. all but a

10. A totem
    a. is a word that comes from the Ojibwa American Indian word that means "he is a relative of mine."
    b. is a symbol of animals, plants, natural forces, and objects.
    c. is usually associated with a clan's concept of its mythical origins.
    d. may be found in our own society in the names we give to baseball and football teams.
    e. all of the above

11. A phratry is a unilineal descent group composed of two or more _____ that believe they are related to each other.
    a. moieties
    b. totems
    c. kindred
    d. lineages
    e. clans

12. Members of a moiety
    a. belong to one of two major descent groups in a society.
    b. are those who are divorced (they lack their "better half").
    c. are usually able to trace their exact genealogical links to their common ancestor.
    d. feel a much stronger feeling of kinship than is felt by members of a lineage or clan.
    e. belong to a group that is smaller than a lineage.

13. A person in a system of bilateral descent
    a. traces descent through the father for some purposes, and through the mother for other purposes.
    b. traces descent through female lines.
    c. traces descent through male lines.
    d. uses totems to symbolically represent the group.
    e. traces descent through both parents simultaneously and recognizes multiple ancestors.

14. Descent groups are frequently found to be important organizing devices in
    a. food-foraging societies.
    b. horticultural societies.
    c. pastoral societies.
    d. intensive agricultural societies.
    e. all of the above except *a*

15. _____ develop out of extended families when families split up and move to nearby regions, and the core members of these families recognize their descent from a common ancestor and continue to organize activities based on this idea.
    a. Phratries
    b. Kindred groups
    c. Lineages
    d. Moieties
    e. Cognatic groups

16. If two people are given the same kinship term, this means that
    a. they have the same genes.
    b. no one can tell the difference between them.
    c. they occupy a similar status.
    d. they are identical twins.
    e. they are members of an adopted family.

17. In _____ kinship terminology, ego's "brother" and "sister" are distinguished from "cousins"; both ego's father's brother and mother's brother are given the same kinship term, "uncle."
    a. Eskimo
    b. Hawaiian
    c. Crow
    d. Omaha
    e. Iroquois

18. In the _____ system of kinship terminology, ego's father, father's brother, and mother's brother are all referred to by the same term, and ego's mother, mother's sister, and father's sister are all referred to by the same term; the term "brother" includes ego's brothers as well as male cousins.
    a. Iroquois
    b. Crow
    c. Omaha
    d. Hawaiian
    e. Eskimo

19. In _____ kinship terminology, the term "brother" is given to ego's brother, father's brother's son, and mother's sister's son; a different term is used for the sons of father's sister and mother's brother. "Mother" refers to ego's mother and mother's sister, "father" refers to ego's father and father's brother. Separate terms are used for ego's mother's brother and father's sister.
    a. Eskimo
    b. Hawaiian
    c. Iroquois
    d. cognatic
    e. kindred

20. The Crow kinship terminology system
    a. is associated with matrilineal descent.
    b. merges paternal cross-cousins with the paternal generation.
    c. is associated with patrilineal descent.
    d. merges maternal cross-cousins with the generation of ego's children.
    e. all but *c*

21. The Omaha kinship terminology system
    a. is associated with partrilineal descent.
    b. merges maternal cross-cousins with the parental generation.
    c. merges paternal cross-cousins with the generation of ego's children.
    d. identifies maternal cross-cousins with the lineage of ego's mother (the lineage that supplies women to ego's patrilineage).
    e. all of the above

22. The descriptive system of kinship terminology _____
    a. gives the same kinship term for ego's mother's brother and father's brother.
    b. is the most common form of kinship terminology.
    c. gives a separate term for each kind of cousin.
    d. is the least precise of all the kinship systems.
    e. indicates that all of ego's siblings have the same social status.

23. Which of the following would NOT be considered typical activities outside the house of a rural Taiwanese woman?
    a. wash clothes on the riverbank
    b. clean and pare vegetables at a communal pump
    c. mend clothes under a tree
    d. stop to rest on a bench with other women
    e. shop at the marketplace

24. In autumn 1981, Dutch anthropologist _____ went to Maine to check out a job at the Association of Aroostook Indians, which needed a research and development director.
    a. Alan Kolata
    b. Fred Plog
    c. Margaret Boone
    d. Weston LaBarre
    e. Harald Prins

25. This major theoretician of nineteenth-century North American anthropology has been regarded as the founder of kinship studies.
    a. Margaret Mead
    b. Leslie White
    c. Julian Steward
    d. Lewis Henry Morgan
    e. Geoffrey Gorer

Answers to multiple-choice practice questions

1. e	8. e	15. c	22. c
2. a	9. e	16. c	23. e
3. b	10. e	17. a	24. e
4. e	11. e	18. d	25. d
5. d	12. a	19. c	
6. e	13. e	20. e	
7. a	14. e	21. e	

True/False Practice Questions

1. Cross-cousins are ideal marriage partners in an arrangement whereby lineages engage in reciprocal marriage exchanges to establish alliances.

2. Omaha kinship terminology is the matrilineal equivalent of the Crow system.

3. The system with the greatest number of kin terms is the Sudanese or Descriptive system.

4. The kindred is a kin group that is organized laterally rather than lineally.

5. The boundaries of a kindred are permanent and definite.

6. Women in rural Taiwan live their lives in the walled courtyards of their husbands' households.

7. It is in their relations in the outside world that women develop sufficient backing to maintain some independence under their powerful mothers-in-law.

8. The shy young Taiwanese girl who enters the village as a bride is examined as frankly and suspiciously by the women as an animal that is up for sale.

9. A Taiwanese girl who gossips freely about the affairs of her husband's household may find herself always on the outside of the group, or worse yet, accused of snobbery.

10. In rural Taiwan women can serve as a powerful protective force for their defenseless younger members, in this way they are a very liberated force in the village.

11. Even older rural Taiwanese women who have raised their sons properly retain little influence over their sons' actions, especially in activities exclusive to men.

12. A Taiwanese woman is subject to an important set of rules, and to be successful she must strictly obey those rules.

13. A truly successful Taiwanese woman is a rugged individualist who has learned to depend largely on herself while appearing to lean on the males in her family.

Answers to true/false practice questions

1. T	5. F	9. T	13. T
2. F	6. F	10. F	
3. T	7. T	11. F	
4. T	8. T	12. F	

Practice Essays

1. Compare and contrast the social organization of the Hopi and the Chinese.

2. Many North American feminists are interested in the concept of matriarchy, sometimes confusing it with or linking it to the matrilineal descent system. Does matrilineality imply matriarchy? Use concrete examples to explore this.

3. Describe a typical woman's life in rural Taiwan from the time she enters her husband's family as a new bride to the time she reaches seniority in his household as a mother-in-law.

4. Describe how women in patrilineal societies like Taiwan actively manipulate the system to their own advantage as best they can.

Chapter 22
Grouping by Sex, Age, Common Interest, and Class

Synopsis

Chapter 22 examines major kinds of nonkin organizations. Groups defined by gender, age and common interest are described. Finally, stratified forms of social organization such as those involving class or caste are presented.

What You Should Learn From This Chapter

1. Understand the functions of nonkin groupings:
   - sex
   - age
   - common interests
2. Know how societies are stratified and the reasons for social divisions.
3. Understand the differences between class and caste-type stratification.

Key Terms

age grade

age set

cousins club

common-interest association

stratified society

egalitarian society

social class

caste

apartheid

verbal evaluation

symbolic indicators

mobility

open-class societies

Review Questions

1. Describe the separate but equal organization of the Iroquois.

2. In what ways is age grouping evidenced in North America?

3. How does one become a member of an age grade?

4. Distinguish between an age group and an age set.

5. Describe the Tiriki age-set system.

6. How and why are common-interest associations formed?

7. Historically, why have women's groups been less common than men's?

8. What functions do women's associations have?

9. What purposes do urban-oriented associations serve?

10. Describe the interstrata relationship in a stratified society.

11. Contrast an egalitarian society with a stratified society.

12. In what ways might a society be stratified?

13. Briefly describe India's caste system.

14. Compare India's caste system to the South African system of apartheid.

15. How might a stratified society beget an outcast group?

16. What are three aspects of a social-class structure?

17. Distinguish between the three ways social class are manifest in society.

18. What is social-impact assessment?

19. What role does religion play in India's caste system?

20. How and why did the Maya develop a stratified society?

Fill-in-the-Blank

1. An age _____ is a category based on age, a stage through which people pass (such as a "teenager").

2. An age _____ is a group of people who move through life stages together (such as "baby boomers").

3. Among the _____ of South America, men and women work, eat, and sleep separately.

4. Common-interest associations used to be called _____ associations.

5. The text suggests that the caste system is present not only in India but also in _____ and _____.

6. A _____ society is one in which members do not share equally in prestige and basic resources.

7. _____ is a special form of social class in which membership is determined by birth and remains fixed for life.

8. In a class society, people are theoretically able to change their class positions through social _____.

Exercise

Briefly identify and locate the following cultures.

1. Iroquois   2. South African

3. Tiriki   4. Maya

Multiple-Choice Practice Questions

1. High rates of rape appear to be associated with societies in which the roles of males and females are highly segregated, and in which there are efforts by males to be dominant over women. If this is true, we would expect the highest rate of rape to occur among the
   a. Ju/'hoansi.
   b. Mundurucu.
   c. Iroquois.
   d. Mbuti.
   e. Hopi.

2. Ambilineal descent groups were a response among Jewish immigrants to urban life in North America. These groups did not recruit on the basis of age. By the late 1930s, their descendants had become so assimilated that they formed new descent groups, called _____, which excluded their parents and grandparents from membership as well as their own children until they reached legal majority or married.
   a. family circles
   b. cousins clubs
   c. age grades
   d. age sets
   e. common-interest associations

3. In literate societies that rely on the written word for accumulated wisdom, elders are often
   a. treated with great respect because of their wisdom.
   b. considered to be as valuable as their weight in gold.
   c. treated like "living libraries" that contain much needed knowledge.
   d. not considered sources of information.
   e. killed when they turn sixty-five years old.

4. The following _____ are passed through by members of North American culture: toddler, teenager, senior citizen.
   a. age grades
   b. age sets
   c. social classes
   d. castes
   e. open classes

5. Which of the following statements about common-interest associations is INCORRECT?
   a. They were originally referred to in the anthropological literature as voluntary associations.
   b. Common-interest associations are more common in hunter-gatherer societies than in urban-industrial societies.
   c. Common-interest associations are intimately associated with world urbanization and increasing social complexity.
   d. Common-interest associations are found in many traditional societies.
   e. Sometimes one can join a common-interest association voluntarily, and sometimes membership is required by law.

6. The text suggests that women's participation in common-interest associations in traditional societies is often less than men's because
   a. women are less sociable than men.
   b. women have no interests in common because they see each other as sexual competitors.
   c. women remain at home, isolated from other women.
   d. men prevent women from joining such groupings.
   e. women have so many opportunities to socialize that they have little need for common-interest associations.

7. In times of rapid social change
   a. common-interest associations decline in significance.
   b. common-interest associations assume the roles and functions formerly held by kinship or age groups.
   c. women form common-interest associations whereas men retain their membership in age and kinship groups.
   d. men are able to adapt whereas women are not.
   e. the role of the elderly becomes more important as the society adjusts to change.

8. A society composed of several groups that differ in their access to resources and prestige is said to be
   a. stratified.
   b. unfair.
   c. immoral.
   d. egalitarian.
   e. open.

9. A/an _____ is a special form of social class in which membership is determined by birth and remains fixed for life.
   a. clan
   b. phratry
   c. common-interest association
   d. age group
   e. caste

10. Symbolic indicators may not always be reliable in helping you assess someone's class status. Which of the following is an example of this?
   a. A common form of recreation of lower-class males is playing pool at the local beer joint.
   b. A con man from a lower-class background wears a tuxedo when he tries to sell you shares in a nonexistent corporation.
   c. According to Emily Post, one can always identify upper-crust families by the presence of a day maid.
   d. Demille O'Hara, striving to return to the simplicity of life as lived by his tribal ancestors, lets his day maid go.
   e. *b* and *d*

11. The ability to change one's class position is known as
   a. open class.
   b. egalitarian.
   c. social mobility.
   d. indicative of common-interest societies.
   e. inevitable.

12. The degree of social mobility in a stratified society is related to
   a. the prevailing kind of family organization.
   b. its ideology.
   c. the number of different common-interest associations it has.
   d. the difference between its richest and poorest classes.
   e. genetic factors.

13. Which of the following could have contributed to the emergence of social stratification?
    a. All human beings want to be looked up to by their fellow members of society.
    b. Certain descent groups may have monopolized activities that turned out to play an important role in their society (such as propitiation of the gods in a horticultural society exposed to unpredictable weather).
    c. An ethnic group with an economic or military advantage (such as knowledge of intensive agriculture or possession of firearms) that enters a foreign territory may become the ruling class within that area.
    d. all of the above
    e. none of the above

14. Among the first groups to be targeted in the genocide that occurred in Rwanda were
    a. human rights activists
    b. university professors
    c. opposition parties
    d. journalists
    e. a, c, and d

15. As the killing spread to the rural areas of Rwanda, it became a program of genocide specifically targeted at the
    a. Hutu
    b. Tutsi
    c. Twa
    d. !Kung San
    e. Kikuyu

16. According to the original study "Genocide in Rwanda," a _____ requires motive, means, and opportunity.
    a. wrong
    b. crime
    c. transgression
    d. atrocity
    e. violation

17. Which of the following are the three main groups in Rwandan society?
    a. the Nuer, Azande, and Mende
    b. the Kapauku, Kaluli, and the Karumba
    c. Twa, Hutu, and Tutsi
    d. Yoruba, Swazi, and Tsembaga
    e. Shuar, Yanomami, and Toda

18. Rwanda was once ruled by what European country?
    a. France
    b. Germany
    c. England
    d. Belgium
    e. Holland

19. Two things enable one to identify an individual as a Twa, Hutu, or Tutsi; they are
    a. knowledge of the person's ancestry
    b. possession of an identity card
    c. height
    d. language
    e. a and b

20. A kind of policy research frequently done by an anthropologists is called a
    a. ethnology
    b. ethnography
    c. participant observation
    d. social impact assessment
    e. need assessment

21. In the U.S., any project requiring a federal permit or license, or using federal funds, by law must be preceded by a
    a. need assessment
    b. archaeological assessment
    c. cultural impact assessment
    d. assessment of feasibility
    e. social impact statement

22. Anthropologist _____ was hired to carry out a social impact assessment of a water diversion project in New Mexico.
    a. Sue Ellen Jacobs
    b. Harald Prins
    c. Alan Kolata
    d. Margaret Boone
    e. Fred Plog

Answers to multiple-choice practice questions

1. b	7. b	13. d	19. e
2. b	8. a	14. e	20. d
3. d	9. e	15. b	21. e
4. a	10. e	16. b	22. a
5. b	11. c	17. c	
6. e	12. a	18. d	

True/False Practice Questions

1. Division of labor by sex is characteristic of all human societies.

2. Usually an increase in the number of common-interest associations is associated with urbanization, but these associations are also found in traditional societies.

3. Castes are strongly exogamous.

4. Mobility refers to the ability to change one's class position.

5. An age grade is a group of people initiated into the group at the same time who move though the series of categories together.

6. According to the original study in your textbook "Genocide in Rwanda," Rwanda has long been known as a true nation in Africa.

7. The three groups in Rwanda the Twa, Hutu, and Tutsi are actually three different strata of the same group.

8. It is easy to tell which group a Rwandan belongs to by his/her height.

9. The major factors in the violence in Rwanda is the fact that the groups involved speak a different language, and have a different culture and religion.

10. Other contributing factors to the violence in Rwanda is that the groups involved live in different places and have a strong sense of tribal pride.

11. The crime of genocide in Rwanda was misdiagnosed by the international community as spontaneous ethnic violence.

12. One of the major objections to the construction of the water diversion project in New Mexico is that it would result in the obliteration of the three-hundred-year-old irrigation system structures.

Answers to true/false practice questions:

1. T	5. F	9. F
2. T	6. T	10. F
3. F	7. T	11. T
4. T	8. F	12. T

Practice Matching

Match the culture with its characteristic.

1. _____ Iroquois

2. _____ Tiriki

3. _____ New York Jews

4. _____ South Africans

5. _____ Maya

a. Cousins clubs in urban immigrant society

b. African nomadic pastoralists with an age set/age grade system

c. Castelike social organization based on racial divisions

d. Native Americans with separate but equal gender organization

e. Stratified society of pre-Columbian Central America

Answers to practice matching

1. d	2. b	3. a	4. c	5. e

Practice Essay

1. Marx felt that religion was "the opiate of the masses," claiming that it was often used by the upper classes to perpetuate their own dominance. Can this perspective be applied to the Indian caste system? Would it be ethnocentric to do so?

2. Describe age grouping in Western society, using as an example the cousins clubs of North America.

3. Because of the nature of Rwandan society, the genocide in Rwanda required a mass mobilization of killers. What is the nature of society in Rwanda? Explain.

4. What were the findings of the social impact assessment of the water diversion project in New Mexico?

Chapter 23
Political Organization and
Maintenance of Order

Synopsis

Chapter 23 defines politics as a system that maintains social order within and between societies. Decentralized and centralized types of political systems are described and an attempt is made to define "law" in cross-cultural terms. The concepts of authority and legitimacy are discussed and various kinds of leadership are examined.

What you should learn from this chapter

1. Know the four major kinds of political organization:
   - bands
   - tribes
   - chiefdoms
   - states
2. Understand how internal political and social control is maintained in different political systems.
3. Understand how external affairs are conducted in different political systems.
4. Understand how conflicts are resolved and the functions of law.
5. Recognize the impact of religion on social control.

Key Terms

political organization

uncentralized system

band

tribe

segmentary lineage system

centralized system

chiefdom

state

nation

sanctions

law

negotiation

mediation

adjudication

world view

Review Questions

1. What are the four basic kinds of political systems?

2. What kinds of societies typically have decentralized systems?

3. How is authority conferred in a band?

4. How is authority conferred in a tribe?

5. Distinguish between the segmentary lineage system and the clan.

6. What is the role of the leopard-skin chief of the Nuer?

7. What is the function of age-grade systems in the political structure of tribes?

8. Describe the role of the *tonowi* among the Kapauku Papuans.

9. What kinds of societies typically have centralized political systems?

10. Distinguish between nation and state.

11. What has women's role generally been in political leadership?

12. Describe women's role in Igbo society.

13. How is social control generally maintained in bands and tribes?

14. How do internalized controls guide behavior?

15. Distinguish between positive and negative sanctions.

16. Distinguish between informal and formal sanctions.

17. What are the limits on power in Bedouin society?

18. Why is the definition of law destined to be inexact?

19. What are the functions of law?

20. Differentiate between negotiation, adjudication, and mediation.

21. How are disputes handled by the Kpelle?

22. Why might warfare be so prominent in food-producing societies?

23. Compare the world view of the Abenaki with that of the Iroquois.

24. Distinguish between force and legitimacy.

25. In what ways is religion connected with politics?

Fill-in-the-Blank

1. The term _____ refers to the system of social relationships that is connected with the maintenance of public order.

2. The term _____ refers to an administrative system having specialized personnel.

3. Anthropologists have identified four types of political systems; two are said to be _____ and two _____.

4. An egalitarian, autonomous small group composed of related people who occupy a single region is called a _____.

5. All humans were food foragers living in band-type organizations until about _____ years ago.

6. The _____ are an example of a society practicing band-level organization.

7. Most conflict in bands is settled by informal means, and decisions are usually made by _____.

8. A _____ is a larger grouping than a band and is linked to a specific territory.

9. A form of political organization in which a larger group is broken up into clans that are then divided into lineages, is called a _____ lineage system.

10. Among the Nuer, the tendency for widespread feuding to occur among lineages is counterbalanced by the actions of the _____.

11. In tribal societies of Melanesia, a type of leader called the _____ or *tonowi* is prevalent.

12. A_____is a ranked society in which every member has a position in the hierarchy.

13. Chiefdoms are linked to _____ economic systems.

14. The Swazi have a _____-level political system.

15. States are typically linked to _____ subsistence patterns.

16. An example of a society in which women play a notably strong political role is the _____.

17. The Wape of New Guinea use belief in _____ as a means of social control.

18. In North America we rely on both external and _____ controls to maintain social order.

19. Among the Bedouin _____ sanctions restrict the inappropriate use of power by those in authority.

20. The Inuit use _____ as a means of resolving conflict.

21. Malinowski distinguished law from _____ by whether there was a "definite social machinery of binding force."

22. Western societies make a distinction between _____ law, involving offenses committed against individuals, and _____ law, involving offenses committed against the state.

23. Disputes may be settled by _____, the use of direct argument and compromise by the disputing parties, or by _____, settlement through the assistance of an unbiased third party.

24. Warfare is most closely linked to the _____-type political system.

Exercises

I. Fill in the chart below, giving examples of each of the major types of political systems and describing their general characteristics. You can use this to study from later.

Types of Political Systems

Type	Example	Characteristics
Band		
Tribe		
Chiefdom		
State		

II. Briefly identify and locate the following cultures.

1. Nuer

2. Kpelle

3. Igbo

4. Bedouin

5. Abenaki

6. Swazi

Multiple-Choice Practice Questions

1. The term "government" may be defined as
   a. a kinship-based age set.
   b. those aspects of social organization concerned with coordination and regulation of public behavior.
   c. the informal leadership of a Ju/'hoansi hunter-gatherer band.
   d. common-interest association focusing on political events.
   e. an administrative system having specialized personnel.

2. Bands and tribes are both
   a. centralized.
   b. associated with industrialism.
   c. dependent on age groups for political organization.
   d. uncentralized and egalitarian.
   e. hierarchical in social organization.

3. The form of social organization typical of hunter-gatherers is the _____, whereas horticulture and pastoralism are usually associated with the form of social organization called the _____.
   a. tribe/chiefdom
   b. tribe/state
   c. tribe/band
   d. band/chiefdom
   e. band/tribe

4. The "leopard-skin chief" among the Nuer
   a. is the head of the largest and most powerful clan.
   b. is the head of the dominant matrilineage.
   c. has the authority to force feuding lineages to accept "blood cattle" and stop feuding.
   d. tries to mediate between feuding sides but does not have political power.
   e. is the totem of one of the Nuer lineages.

5. Age-grade systems and common-interest associations are effective methods of integrating small autonomous units such as bands into larger social units. These methods may be described as _____ systems of political organization.
   a. segmentary
   b. negotiated
   c. state
   d. nonkinship
   e. kinship

6. A _____ is a ranked society in which every member has a position in the hierarchy, and an individual's status is determined by membership in a descent group.
   a. band
   b. tribe
   c. chiefdom
   d. state
   e. kindred

7. The state is distinctive in the extensiveness of its legitimate use of _____ to regulate the affairs of its citizens.
   a. kinship
   b. force
   c. chiefs
   d. religion
   e. gossip

8. In a chiefdom, an individual's status is determined by membership in a
   a. government.
   b. social class.
   c. bureaucracy.
   d. descent group.
   e. secret society.

9. A cross-cultural comparison of systems of political organization reveals that
   a. many women who hold high office do so by virtue of their relationship to men.
   b. many women in positions of leadership adopt characteristics of temperament that are usually considered masculine.
   c. in many societies, women have as much political power as men.
   d. women may play an important role in political decisions even when they are not visible public leaders.
   e. All but *c*

10. At the heart of political organization is
    a. control of unacceptable social behavior.
    b. the legitimate use of force to maintain order.
    c. unequal access to power.
    d. the dominance of males over females.
    e. the development of egalitarian relationships.

11. Sanctions refer to
    a. internalized social controls.
    b. holy behavior.
    c. externalized social controls.
    d. decadent behavior.
    e. ritualized behavior.

12. _____ sanctions attempt to precisely and explicitly regulate people's behavior. They can be positive (such as military decorations) or negative (such as imprisonment).
    a. Hierarchical
    b. Egalitarian
    c. Informal
    d. Formal
    e. Magical

13. In centralized societies, antisocial behavior is usually dealt with in a court system by the use of formal, negative sanctions involving the application of abstract rules and the use of force. The primary aim is
    a. to help the victim.
    b. to renew social relations between the victim and the perpetrator of the crime.
    c. to prevent witchcraft from being used.
    d. to assign and punish guilt.
    e. to provide a good show for the spectators.

14. The functions of law include
    a. the definition of proper behavior in particular circumstances so that everyone is clear about their rights and duties.
    b. protecting the wealthy from the poor.
    c. redefining what is proper behavior when situations change.
    d. allocating authority to use coercion to enforce sanctions.
    e. All but *b*

15. A method of resolving disputes in which the disputing parties voluntarily arrive at a mutually satisfactory agreement is called
    a. negotiation.
    b. mediation.
    c. adjudication.
    d. use of sanctions.
    e. law.

16. Which of the following are likely to be associated with warfare?
    a. centralized political systems
    b. the rise of cities
    c. a technology that supports population growth
    d. possession of complex, valuable property
    e. All of the above

17. An exploitative world view is more likely to exist in which of the following technologies?
    a. Food foraging
    b. Horticulture
    c. Pastoralism
    d. Intensive agriculture
    e. All of the above except *a*

18. Power based on force does not usually last very long; to be effective, it must be considered
    a. legitimate.
    b. mediated.
    c. negotiated.
    d. subject to sanctions.
    e. inevitable.

19. _____, which seem to be associated with the weak and with dependents, provides one of several checks on the abuse of authority in Bedouin society.
    a. Ostracism
    b. Informal sanctions
    c. Legal sanctions
    d. Paralegal sanctions
    e. Supernatural sanctions

20. Another agent of control in societies, whether or not they possess centralized political systems, may be _____.
    a. witchcraft.
    b. sorcerers.
    c. ostracism.
    d. fines set by judges.
    e. warriors.

21. An important pioneer in the anthropological study of law was _____.
    a. A. L. Kroeber.
    b. George Peter Murdock.
    c. John Wesley Powell.
    d. E. Adamson Hoebel.
    e. Peggy Reeves Sanday.

22. The field of _____ is one of growing anthropological
    involvement and employment.
    a. ethnoscience
    b. ethnology
    c. dispute control
    d. dispute management
    e. assertiveness training

23. In 1980, _____as a practitioner of dispute management, helped the U.S. and
    the Soviet Union replace their obsolete "hot line" with fully equipped nuclear crisis
    centers in each capital.
    a. Sue Ellen Jacobs
    b. William L. Ury
    c. Margaret Boone
    d. Alan Kolata
    e. Harald Prins

Answers to multiple-choice practice questions

1. e	7. b	13. d	20. a
2. d	8. d	14. e	21. d
3. e	9. e	15. a	22. d
4. d	10. a	16. e	23. b
5. d	11. c	17. e	
6. c	12. d	18. a	

True/False Practice Questions

1. In the French monarchy under Louis XIV, the king *was* the state in an important sense.

2. Until recently many non-Western peoples had no fixed form of government in the
   sense that Westerners understand the term.

3. The Ju/'hoansi have a tribal-type political organization.

4. The Big Man of the Kapauku is called *tonowi*.

5. A classic example of a segmentary lineage system is found among the Nuer.

6. In Bedouin society, because those in authority are expected to treat their dependents with some respect, they must draw as little attention as possible to the inequality of their relationship.

7. The use of fictive kin terms serves to mask relations of inequality in Bedouin society.

8. Among the Bedouins, the tyranny of those in power is accepted as natural and tolerated.

9. A Bedouin woman can resist a tyrannical husband by leaving for her natal home "angry." This is the approved response to abuse in Bedouin society.

10. Bedouin women have less recourse against tyrannical fathers or guardians, but various informal means to resist the imposition of unwanted decisions do exist, although suicide is not one of them.

11. Figures of authority in Bedouin society are vulnerable to their dependents because their positions rest on the respect these people are willing to give them.

12. What anthropologists involved with dispute management are trying to do is to help create a culture of negotiation in a world where adversarial, win-lose attitudes are out of step with the increasingly interdependent relations between people.

Answers to true/false practice questions

1. T	4. T	7. T	10. F
2. F	5. T	8. F	11. T
3. F	6. T	9. T	12. T

Practice Matching

Match the culture with its characteristic.

1. _____ Nuer

2. _____ Swazi

3. _____ Igbo

4. _____ Wape

5. _____ Abenaki

a. Nigerian society in which men and women occupy separate political spheres

b. Northeastern Native American foragers in the historic past that lived in harmony with their environment

c. A southeast African state

d. A New Guinea people in the historical past with effective informal and internalized controls

e. East African herders with a segmentary lineage system

Answers to practice matching

1. e   2. e   3. a   4. d   5. b

Practice Essay

1. Why has the state-type system expanded to encompass most of the globe today? Explore how band, tribe, and chiefdom organizations might persist within a world order based primarily on states.

2. Identify and discuss the limits on the power of authority figures in Bedouin society. That is, what options are open to dependents in Bedouin society that would allow them to check an oppressive authority figure.

Chapter 24
Religion and the Supernatural

Synopsis

In Chapter 24 the textbook discusses the universality of religion, considering the functions served by religious belief and ritual in the social order. Various kinds of supernatural beings are compared and the relationships among magic, science, and religion are examined. The role of religion in culture change is also discussed.

What you should learn from this chapter

1. Understand why religion exists.
2. Understand the various forms of religious belief:
   - animatism
   - animism
   - shamanism
   - belief in ancestral spirits
   - belief in gods and goddesses
3. Understand the relationship between religion, magic, and witchcraft and the functions of each.
4. Understand the role of religion in cultural change.

Key Terms and Names

religion

pantheon

Edward B. Tylor

animism

animatism

priest or priestess

shaman

rites of passage

rites of intensification

separation

transition

incorporation

imitative magic

contagious magic

witchcraft

divination

revitalization movements

Review Questions

1. What is the relationship between science and religion?

2. Why might there be less religion, as defined in your textbook, in more complex societies?

3. What are three categories of supernatural beings?

4. What is the role of gods and goddesses in many societies?

5. How does healing occur among the Ju/'hoansi?

6. What purpose do ancestral spirits serve?

7. In what type of society is one likely to find animism?

8. Distinguish between animism and animatism.

9. How does mana perpetuate itself?

10. In what type of society is one likely to find priestesses?

11. How are shamans made and how do they carry out their work?

12. What benefits do people derive from enlisting the services of a shaman?

13. What are two main types of ritual?

14. What are the three stages in a rite of passage, according to Van Gennep?

15. Why are rites of intensification performed?

16. Distinguish between the two fundamental principles of magic.

17. In what ways does the Tewa origin myth reflect Tewa social structure?

18. How are witch hunts used for societal control?

19. What is the role of witchcraft among the Navajo?

20. What are the psychological functions of religion?

21. What are the social functions of religion?

22. How and why do revitalization movements emerge?

Fill-in-the-Blank

1. Alfonso Ortiz was an anthropologist of _____ ancestry who studied the religious beliefs of the Tewa.

2. In Tewa society the _____ mediate between the human and spiritual worlds and between the two moieties.

3. In the nineteenth century European thinkers believed that _____ would eventually eclipse religion.

4. The set of gods and goddesses in a society are called its _____.

5. In most societies with subsistence bases in _____ or _____, deities are conceptualized as masculine.

6. A belief that nature is animated by spirits is called _____.

7. A concept of impersonal power, such as mana, is called _____.

8. _____ are specialists who have acquired spiritual power, which they can use on behalf of human clients.

9. _____ was a pioneer in the study of rites of passage.

10. When Mende girls are initiated into adult society, they undergo _____.

11. A ceremony to bring rain to a drought-stricken community is a _____.

12. The three stages of a life crisis ritual are _____, _____, and _____.

13. _____ wrote *The Golden Bough.*

14. _____ magic is based on the assumption that things that are similar to each other have an effect on each other.

15. Assuming that a person's fingernail clippings, hair, blood, and so on retain a spiritual connection to that person is the basis for _____ magic.

16. Among the Navajo, _____ is a way of expression and channeling hostile feelings.

17. A _____ is a social movement whose intent is to totally transform a society.

18. Anthropologist _____ studied the stages typical of revitalization movements.

Exercise

Briefly identify and locate the following cultures discussed in the chapter.

1. Tewa

2. Sioux

3. Ibibio

4. Mende

Multiple-Choice Practice Questions

1. Islamic fundamentalism in Iran and Christian fundamentalism in the United States demonstrate that
   a. science has succeeded in destroying religion in the twentieth century.
   b. religious activity is prominent in the lives of social elites.
   c. science meets basic needs.
   d. religion is a powerful and dynamic force in society today.
   e. science is wrong.

2. _____ may be defined as the beliefs and patterns of behavior by which people try to control those aspects of the universe that are otherwise beyond their control.
   a. Political organization
   b. Government
   c. Kinship
   d. Common-interest associations
   e. Religion

3. Which of the following is LEAST likely to be extensively involved in religious beliefs and activities?
   a. single women with ten children, living below the poverty line and who dropped out of school at age fourteen
   b. members of food-foraging societies with limited scientific knowledge
   c. peasants in a feudal society
   d. members of lower classes in an urban-industrial society
   e. wealthy members of urban-industrial societies with advanced scientific knowledge

4. A people's collection of gods and goddesses is called a
   a. mana.
   b. shaman.
   c. pantheon.
   d. priest.
   e. fetish.

5. Belief in a supreme being who controls the universe is usually associated with
   a. bands.
   b. tribes.
   c. chiefdoms.
   d. states.
   e. multinational corporations.

6. If religious belief reflects the structure of society, in which types of society would you expect to find widespread belief in ancestral spirits?
   a. those in which descent groups play a major role in social organization
   b. those with a disproportionately large number of old people
   c. those with a disproportionately large number of young people
   d. those in which neolocal marital residence is the rule
   e. those with egocentric systems such as the kindred

7. The belief that nature is animated with spirits is called
   a. animation.
   b. anima.
   c. animatism.
   d. animism.
   e. ennui.

8. A _____ is a full-time religious specialist who occupies an office that has a certain rank and function.
   a. shaman
   b. priest
   c. witch
   d. magician
   e. diviner

9. In acting as a healer, the shaman
   a. accurately diagnoses medical problems.
   b. may improve the patient's state of mind, which aids in recovery.
   c. may be coping with his or her own problems by becoming intensely involved with the problems of others.
   d. provides reassurance to the community through an elaborate drama that may involve trickery.
   e. All but *a*

10. Ceremonies such as bar mitzvah, elaborate wedding ceremonies, baby showers, and graduation parties that help individuals make major changes in their lives are referred to as rites of
    a. transition.
    b. intensification.
    c. separation.
    d. passage.
    e. incorporation.

11. A funeral ceremony may be regarded as
    a. a rite of passage.
    b. an opportunity to restore the equilibrium of the group.
    c. an opportunity for individuals to express their feelings in a structured way that ensures continuation of society.
    d. a rite of intensification.
    e. All of the above

12. In *The Golden Bough,* _____ distinguished between religion and magic.
    a. Bronislaw Malinowski
    b. Franz Boas
    c. Sir James Frazer
    d. Sir Edward Tylor
    e. Clifford Geertz

13. Many magical incantations require the use of fingernail clippings of the intended victim. This is an example of
    a. imitative magic.
    b. contagious magic.
    c. witch magic.
    d. nightmare magic.
    e. scientific thinking.

14. Magic involves the manipulation of powers for good or evil, whereas witchcraft involves the possession of an innate power used for
    a. religious purposes.
    b. scientific reasons.
    c. evil.
    d. traditional societies.
    e. societies that lack religion.

15. Religion, magic, and witchcraft are all SIMILAR in which of the following ways?
    a. They all disappear once modern education and scientific training expand.
    b. They all share the common goal of improving social relationships within a community.
    c. They are all associated with morose nonconformists who try to destroy society.
    d. They provide explanations of events and are mechanisms of social control.
    e. They are all morally neutral.

16. A belief in _____ enables people to explain why things go wrong by blaming certain individuals who are said to have the internal psychic ability to cause harm to others.
    a. witchcraft
    b. magic
    c. divination
    d. contagion
    e. evil

17. Which of the following illustrate the psychological functions of religion?
    a. Among the Holy Ghost People of the United States, handling snakes and drinking strychnine is a common feature of their worship; one explanation of this behavior is that by confronting the possibility of death, they achieve a sense of awe and transcendence.
    b. An Islamic judge who orders the hand of a thief cut off can sleep soundly at night because he thinks of himself as merely the agent of divinely inspired justice.
    c. The Tewa Indian origin myth provides every Tewa with a sense of this place in an orderly universe.
    d. A person raised in the Catholic religion feels tremendous guilt when she/he commits a wrong.
    e. All but *d*

18. A _____ is a deliberate effort by members of a society to construct a more satisfying culture.
    a. divination
    b. rite of intensification
    c. fetish
    d. segmentary lineage system
    e. revitalization movement

19. Which of the following statements about revitalization movements is INCORRECT?
    a. The purpose of revitalization movements is to reform society.
    b. Revitalization movements always fail because they require too much change to be tolerated.
    c. All known major religions, including Judaism, Christianity, and Islam, began as revitalization movements.
    d. Revitalization movements may be completely unrealistic.
    e. Revitalization movements may be adaptive and give rise to long-lasting religions.

20. *N/um* generally remains dormant in a healer until an effort is made to activate it. Among the ways to activate *n/um* are
   a. trance dance.
   b. hallucinogenic drugs.
   c. medicinal curing ceremony.
   d. solo singing.
   e. All but *b*

21. In southern Africa's Swaziland all types of illnesses are generally thought to be caused by _____ or _____.
   a. viruses/bacteria
   b. negative karma/negative attitude
   c. sorcery/loss of ancestral protection
   d. poor hygiene/poverty
   e. None of the above

22. Which of the following have the Swazi NOT traditionally relied upon for treatment of disease?
   a. herbalists
   b. diviner mediums
   c. Christian faith healers
   d. general practitioners
   e. they rely on all of the above

23. In a country where there is one traditional healer for every 110 people, but only one physician for every 10,000, the potential benefit of cooperation between physicians and healers seems self-evident. However, it was unrecognized until proposed by anthropologist _____.
   a. Edward C. Green
   b. Harald Prins
   c. Alan Kolata
   d. William L. Ury
   e. Margaret Boone

Answers to multiple-choice practice questions

1. d	7. d	13. b	19. b
2. e	8. b	14. c	20. e
3. e	9. e	15. d	21. c
4. c	10. d	16. a	22. d
5. d	11. e	17. e	23. a
6. a	12. c	18. e	

True/False Practice Questions

1. The belief that nature is animated by spirits is called animism.

2. Rituals reinforce social solidarity and thus enable individuals and groups to get through crisis.

3. Rites of intensification help individuals get through a crisis.

4. Religion provides an orderly model of the universe and reduces fear and anxiety.

5. Interceding with the spirits and drawing out their invisible arrows is the task of (Ju/'hoansi) healers.

6. Among the Ju/'hoansi only men can possess the powerful healing force called *n/um*.

7. *N/um* is the Ju/'hoansi equivalent of *mana*.

8. The trances that healers go into are considered harmless; they simply lose consciousness.

9. The power of healers' *n/um* is all that is thought to protect the healer in a trance from actual death.

10. Today biomedical germ theory is universally accepted in societies around the world.

Answers to true/false practice questions

1. T	5. T	9. T
2. T	6. F	10. F
3. F	7. T	
4. T	8. F	

Practice Matching

Match the culture with its characteristic.

1. _____ Navajo

2. _____ Tewa

3. _____ Ibibio

4. _____ Sioux

5. _____ Mende

a. West African people who practice female initiation rite involving clitoridectomy

b. Southwestern Native Americans with a witchcraft tradition.

c. Native Americans of the plains who started the Ghost Dance as a religious revitalization.

d. Native Americans of New Mexico whose origin myth reflects and validates their social structure.

e. Sub-Saharan African people with a witchcraft tradition

Answers to practice matching

1. b   2. d   3. e   4. c   5. a

Practice Essay

1. Bronislaw Malinowski, in his classic essay *Magic, Science, and Religion,* claimed that each of these was a viable mode of cognition and that most societies exhibit all of them in variable proportions. In what ways does magical thinking persist in contemporary North America? Is it likely to persist into the future?

2. Identify and describe the various ways the Jo/'hoansi activate the powerful healing force called *n/um.*

3. How is modern medicine reconciled with traditional beliefs in Swaziland?

Chapter 25
The Arts

Synopsis

Chapter 25 examines the ethnocentric assumptions implicit in most Western definitions of the arts and artists. It distinguishes different types of creative activity such as the verbal arts, music, and sculpture and attempts to come up with a cross-culturally valid definition of art.

What you should learn from this chapter

1. Understand why anthropologists are interested in the arts.
2. Understand the forms of verbal arts and how they function in society:
   - myth
   - legend
   - tale
3. Understand the function of music.
4. Understand the range of visual and plastic arts in human societies.

Key Terms

folklore

folkloristics

myth

legend

epic

tale

motif

ethnomusicology

tonality

entopic phenomena

construal

iconic images

Review Questions

1. Distinguish between secular and religious art.

2. What are the basic kinds of verbal arts studied by anthropologists?

3. Give an example of how myth expresses the world view of a people.

4. Distinguish between legend and myth.

5. Why is matriarchy a common theme in many societies' myths?

6. What role does poetry play in the lives of the Bedouins?

7. What type of society is likely to have epics? Why?

8. What aspects of legends are of interest to anthropologists?

9. Why are anthropologists interested in tales?

10. What are the functions of music?

11. Distinguish between art and craft.

12. What is the importance of entopic phenomena?

13. What is the "second stage" of trance?

14. Are there any universal characteristics of art?

Fill-in-the-Blank

1. The term "verbal arts" is preferred to the term _____, a term developed in the 19th century to refer to traditional oral stories of European peasants.

2. The word "myth," in _____ usage, refers to something that is widely believed to be true but isn't.

3. Tabaldak and Odziozo are characters in the origin myth of the _____.

4. Legends are _____ narratives that recount the deeds of heroes, the movements of people, and the establishment of customs.

5. Studies of tales in the southeast United States now indicate that they originated in _____ rather than Europe.

6. "Little songs" that occur every day were studied among the _____.

7. The study of music in its cultural setting is called _____.

8. The term _____ is used to refer to scale systems and their modifications in music.

9. An alternative to the Western octave system is the _____, which is defined by five equidistant tones.

10. Two people playing different patterns of beats at the same time is called _____.

11. The cultures of _____ have a particularly rich tradition of sculpture.

12. Among the Pomo Indians of California, _____ is an important expression of aesthetic interest.

13. The human nervous system produces images out of which patterns are construed. These are called _____.

Multiple-Choice Practice Questions

1. Whether useful or non-useful, all art is an expression of
   a. the innate need to be impractical.
   b. a fundamental human capacity for religious expression.
   c. state-level societies that can afford specialists.
   d. political domination of minorities by elites.
   e. the symbolic representation of form and the expression of feeling that constitutes creativity.

2. The observation that all cultures include activities that provide aesthetic pleasure suggests that
   a. humans may have an innate or acquired need to produce art.
   b. the human mind requires the stimulation of imaginative play to prevent boredom.
   c. all societies, from food-foraging bands to industrial states, include art in their culture.
   d. art is a necessary activity in which all normal, active members of society participate.
   e. All of the above

3. Anthropologists prefer to use the term *verbal arts* rather than the term *folklore* because the term
   a. *folklore* is used only by linguists; the term *verbal arts* is used only by anthropologists.
   b. *verbal arts* sounds more sophisticated.
   c. *verbal arts* is more scientific.
   d. *folklore* implies lack of sophistication and is a condescending term to use.
   e. *folklore* refers only to fairy tales.

4. The type of verbal arts that has received the most study and attention is
   a. poetry.
   b. incantations.
   c. narratives.
   d. proverbs.
   e. riddles.

5. In the myth of Tabaldak and Odziozo, Tabaldak first created the Abenakis from stone and then from living wood. What does this tell us about the functions of myth?
   a. Myths function to tell actual history; the Abenakis believe that they were originally made of wood.
   b. Myths bring humor into the lives of the Abenakis because the myths are so ridiculous.
   c. Myths function primarily to provide entertainment; the Abenakis know they were not made from wood, but like to tell this story to visiting anthropologists who are so gullible.
   d. Myths function to express a culture's world view; the Abenakis see themselves as belonging to the world of living things rather than to the nonliving world of stone.
   e. Myths provide skills of woodworking and stone masonry to the Abenakis.

6. Because legends contain details of a people's past, they are a form of history; because they often give a picture of a people's view of the world and humanity's place in it, they are like
   a. poetry.
   b. religion.
   c. magic.
   d. kinship systems.
   e. myths.

7. When an anthropologist uses the term _____, he or she is referring to a category of verbal narratives that are secular, non-historical, and seen primarily as a source of entertainment.
   a. "folklore"
   b. "myth"
   c. "tale"
   d. "legend"
   e. "drama"

8. Your text describes a type of narrative found in many cultures in which a peasant father and his son, while traveling with their beast of burden, meet a number of people who criticize them. What is the motif?
   a. The "motif" refers to the psychological motives of the characters in a story, in this case the desire of the son to do better than his father.
   b. "Motif" means the historical background to the story, in this case the history of exploitation of the peasantry.
   c. The "motif" refers to the story situation, in this case a father and son trying to please everyone.
   d. "Motif" means the physical environment in which the story occurs, in this case the yam gardens of Ghana.
   e. The "motif" refers to the economic background, in this case feudalism.

9. The "little songs" of the Bedouin are considered un-Islamic; they are the discourse of children, used to express rebellious ideas and feelings. Thus they are
   a. anti-structural.
   b. forbidden.
   c. sung among Europeans only.
   d. sung only when the Bedouins are away from their homeland.
   e. sung only at marriages.

10. The field of ethnomusicology
    a. is concerned with human music rather than natural music.
    b. is the study of music in its cultural setting.
    c. began in the 19th century with the collection of folk songs.
    d. concerns the organization of melody, rhythm, and form in a culture's music.
    e. All of the above

11. Scale systems and their modifications in music are called
    a. tonality.
    b. ethnomusicology.
    c. sculpture.
    d. verbal arts.
    e. pentatonic.

12. During the Washington Peace March in the '60s, thousands of people sang the song "We Shall Overcome." This song expressed a feeling of common purpose to counteract repression and to reform society. It created a sense of unity among diverse members of the crowd. This example illustrates the _____ of music.
    a. social functions
    b. geographical distribution
    c. tonality
    d. mythological features
    e. polyrhythms

13. Objects that are trivial, low in symbolic content, or impermanent are usually considered products of
    a. an ethnomusicologist.
    b. a tale.
    c. craft.
    d. art.
    e. sculpture.

14. Amongst the Kalahari groups of the 1950s and 1960s, about half the men and a third of the women were _____.
    a. rock artists.
    b. shaman.
    c. hunters.
    d. gatherers.
    e. chiefs.

15. For this group of Native Americans basket-making has been important for their sense of who they are since before European contact.
    a. Cheyenne
    b. Hurok
    c. Pomo
    d. Chumash
    e. Comanche

16. After comprehensive archaeological, ethnographic, and other studies were completed in 1976, anthropologist _____ succeeded in having the Pomo basketry materials recognized by the National Register of Historic Places as "historic property."
    a. Richard N. Lerner
    b. Edward C. Green
    c. Alan Kolata
    d. William L. Ury
    e. Margaret Boone

Answers to multiple-choice practice questions

1. e	5. d	9. a	13. c
2. e	6. e	10. e	14. b
3. d	7. c	11. a	15. c
4. c	8. c	12. a	16. a

True/False Practice Questions

1. The term "tale" refers to a type of narrative that is secular, non-historical, and seen primarily as a source of entertainment.

2. Legends are semi-historical narratives that recount the deeds of heroes, the movement of peoples and the establishment of local customs.

3. The word "myth," in popular usage, refers to something that is widely believed to be true but probably isn't.

4. Legends provide clues as to what is considered appropriate behavior in a culture.

5. Bushman rock images are banal, meaningless artifacts akin to urban graffiti in the U.S.

6. Bushman art has a single, one-to-one "meaning" that it unequivocally transmits from the maker to the viewer.

7. Bushman rock art were simply records of religious experiences.

8. Bushman rock art were not just pictures, but rather powerful things in themselves that could facilitate the mediation of the cosmological realms.

9. Bushman rock art were just pictures that had no power to effect changes in the shamans' states of consciousness.

10. The making of art was, for the Bushman, an idle pastime.

11. For centuries shamans had fought in the spiritual realm with marauding shamans of illness, so, their art suggests, did they battle in the spiritual realm with the colonists.

12. Bushman rock art itself and the belief system in which it was embedded is much more complex than was ever thought.

Answers to true/false practice questions

1. T	4. T	7. F	10. F
2. T	5. F	8. T	11. T
3. T	6. F	9. F	12. T

Practice Essay

1. Many famous biographies or novels about artists in the West stress the individual creativity of the artist (for example, James Joyce's *Portrait of the Artist as a Young Man*). Artists are portrayed as people who have the vision to rise above and beyond the social and cultural conditions into which they were born, sometimes even crossing the boundaries of normality as typically defined by society. How is this vision of the artist different from the conception of artists held by non-Western societies?

2. Discuss art's general meaning. What is art's role in Bushman communities?

3. Bushman rock art extends beyond the generation of religious experience to the negotiation of political power. Demonstrate why this is so.

4. Discuss why it is important to protect the cultural heritages of tribal peoples. Why is it of concern to anthropologists?

Chapter 26
Cultural Change

Synopsis

Chapter 26 discusses the mechanisms of cultural change and examines anthropology's role in the changes sweeping the world. The use of the term "modernization" is considered from a cross-cultural perspective.

What you should learn from this chapter

1. Understand how cultures change and the mechanisms involved:
   - innovation
   - diffusion
   - cultural loss
   - acculturation
2. Understand why the field of applied anthropology developed.
3. Understand how societies react to forcible change:
   - syncretism
   - revitalization movements
4. Understand the process of modernization and its effect on societies.

Key Terms and Names

primary innovation

secondary innovation

diffusion

acculturation

genocide

applied anthropology

Franz Boas

syncretism

nativistic (revivalistic) movement

modernization

structural differentiation

revolutionary

integrative mechanism

tradition

Review Questions

1. Distinguish between primary and secondary innovation.

2. Provide an example of primary innovation.

3. Why is it that cultural context provides the means for innovation to occur?

4. What things have European Americans borrowed from American Indians?

5. What is meant by cultural loss?

6. Describe the nature of acculturation.

7. What three factors seem to be underlying causes of genocide?

8. What does the field of applied anthropology attempt to accomplish?

9. How did the Trobriand Islanders react to the British game of cricket?

10. What is the purpose of revitalization movements?

11. What are the precipitators of rebellion and revolution?

12. What is the problem with the term "modernization"?

13. What are the four subprocesses of modernization?

14. What is meant by the "culture of discontent"?

Fill-in-the-Blank

1. Innovations based on the chance discovery of some new principle are called _____ innovations, while innovations resulting from the deliberate application of these principles are called _____ innovations.

2. The spread of customs or practices from one culture to another is called _____.

3. According to Ralph Linton, as much as _____ percent of a culture's content is due to borrowing.

4. _____ occurs when groups with different cultures come into intensive, firsthand contact and one or both groups experience massive cultural changes.

5. One society may retain its culture but lose its autonomy, becoming a _____ within the dominant culture.

6. The extermination of one people by another is called _____.

7. The field of _____ anthropology uses anthropological knowledge and techniques for practical purposes.

8. The applied work of anthropologist _____ helped reform the U.S. government's immigration policies.

9. Under conditions of acculturation, indigenous populations may blend foreign traits with those of their own culture to form a new cultural system. This response is called _____.

10. The Trobrianders blended indigenous traditions with the British game of _____.

11. _____ movements are deliberate attempts by members of a society to construct a more satisfactory culture.

12. A revitalization movement that attempts to bring back a destroyed but not forgotten way of life is called a _____ or revivalistic movement.

13. A revitalization movement that attempts to resurrect a suppressed, outcast group that has its own special subcultural ideology and has occupied an inferior social position for a long time is called _____.

14. Revolutions have occurred only during the last _____ years, since the emergence of centralized systems of political authority.

15. Modernization refers to the process of cultural and socioeconomic change whereby developing societies become more similar to _____ industrialized societies.

16. The _____ aspect of modernization means a shift in population from rural areas to cities.

17. The Skolt Lapps in the country of _____ traditionally supported themselves by fishing and reindeer herding.

18. The Shuar Indians promoted cooperative _____ ranching as their new economic base.

19. By the early 1970s the United States, encompassing 6 percent of the world's population, was consuming about _____ percent of the world's output of copper, coal, and oil.

20. The Wauja are a community of indigenous people whose claim to certain lands and the ceremonies that take place there are threatened by _____ and _____.

Exercise

Briefly identify and locate the following cultures.

1. Skolt Lapps

2. Shuar

3. Haitians

4. Wauja

Multiple-Choice Practice Questions

1. In New England, the culture of English speakers replaced the various cultures of Native Americans living along the coast. Your text says that this occurred because
   a. English-speaking culture was superior to Native American culture.
   b. Native American culture was superior to English-speaking culture.
   c. it is inevitable that English speakers will replace other cultures that they encounter.
   d. a combination of accidental factors contributed to the success of English speakers in establishing colonies along coastal New England.
   e. the success of English speakers was only a temporary setback for the progressive development of Native American culture.

2. The chance discovery of some new principle that can be applied in a variety of ways is called
   a. primary innovation.
   b. primary syncretism.
   c. applied anthropology.
   d. millenarism.
   e. diffusion.

3. The deliberate use of basic ideas in some practical application, such as making use of the knowledge of how electricity works to develop the telephone, is called
   a. revitalization.
   b. millenarism.
   c. modernization.
   d. integrative mechanism.
   e. secondary innovation.

4. Copernicus's discovery that the earth orbits the sun rather than vice versa
   a. was a primary innovation that met the cultural goals and needs of his time.
   b. was a primary innovation that was out of step with the needs, values, and goals of the time.
   c. was a secondary innovation that put into application the discovery by Ptolemy that heavenly bodies moved on crystalline spheres around the earth.
   d. was a secondary innovation that was deliberately developed by Copernicus to destroy the Polish Church.
   e. resulted from diffusion of ideas from India.

5. According to the North American anthropologist Ralph Linton, about 90 percent of any culture's content comes from
   a. primary innovation.
   b. diffusion.
   c. invention.
   d. syncretism.
   e. revolution.

6. In biblical times, chariots and carts were widespread in the Middle East, but by the sixth century the roads had deteriorated so much that wheeled vehicles were replaced by camels. This illustrates that cultural change is sometimes due to
   a. primary invention.
   b. secondary invention.
   c. diffusion.
   d. revitalization.
   e. cultural loss.

7. As a result of prolonged firsthand contact between societies A and B, which of the following might happen?
   a. Society A might wipe out society B, with it becoming a new dominant society.
   b. Society A might retain its distinctive culture but lose its autonomy and come to survive as a subculture such as a caste or ethnic group.
   c. Society A might be wiped out by society B, with only a few scattered refugees living as members of the dominant society.
   d. The cultures of A and B might fuse, becoming a single culture with elements of both.
   e. All but *a*

8. The extermination of one group of people by another, often deliberately and in the name of progress, is called
   a. genocide.
   b. acculturation.
   c. diffusion.
   d. applied anthropology.
   e. primary innovation.

9. The field of applied anthropology developed
   a. through efforts to help the poor in North American society.
   b. in sociology classrooms.
   c. in industry.
   d. in colonial situations.
   e. through the efforts of women opposed to prohibition.

10. In acculturation, subordinate groups will often incorporate new cultural elements into their own culture, creating a blend of old and new; a reinterpretation of new cultural elements to fit them with already existing traditions is called
    a. syncretism.
    b. innovation.
    c. diffusion.
    d. integrative mechanism.
    e. modernization.

11. A deliberate attempt by members of society to construct a more satisfying culture may be called
    a. a secondary innovation.
    b. a revitalization movement.
    c. an enervating movement.
    d. syncretism.
    e. a primary innovation.

12. Which of the following is/are considered to be important precipitators of rebellion and revolution?
    a. A sudden reversal of recent economic advances.
    b. The media no longer support the government.
    c. The established leadership loses prestige.
    d. A strong, charismatic leader organizes attacks on the existing government.
    e. All of the above

13. The term "modernization"
    a. is a relativistic rather than ethnocentric concept.
    b. refers to the process of cultural and socioeconomic change whereby societies acquire the characteristics of industrialized societies.
    c. refers to a global and all-encompassing process whereby modern cities gradually deteriorate.
    d. can be used to show that all societies go through the same stages of evolutionary development, culminating in the urban-industrial state.
    e. is not used by anthropologists.

14. As modernization occurs, which of the following changes are likely to follow?
    a. Literacy increases.
    b. Religion decreases.
    c. Kinship plays a less significant role.
    d. Social mobility increases.
    e. All of the above

15. The division of a single role (which serves several functions) into two or more roles (each with a single specialized function) is called
    a. millenarization.
    b. modernization.
    c. structural differentiation.
    d. industrialization.
    e. diffusion.

16. Changes in Skolt Lapp society occurred because
    a. men switched from reindeer herding to other sources of income.
    b. the number of reindeer declined.
    c. snowmobiles were used to herd reindeer.
    d. society became hierarchical.
    e. women became more powerful than men.

17. The indigenous people whom Pedro Alvares Cabral encountered in his "discovery" of Brazil in 1500.
    a. Yanomami
    b. Shuar
    c. Mekranoti
    d. Pataxo
    e. Inca

18. The Brazilian Indian service.
    a. BIA
    b. FOIRN
    c. NGOs
    d. FUNAI
    e. CIMI

19. _____ are street beggars that wander the streets in all major cities of Brazil.
    a. Fandango
    b. Pobres
    c. Mendingo
    d. Gente de las calles
    e. Gente sin casas

20. The most common pattern characterizing violence against indigenous people in Brazil is _____.
    a. racism.
    b. impunity (guilty party gets away with crime).
    c. massacres.
    d. illegal detention.
    e. police brutality.

21. When foreigners go to Haiti, one of the things that impresses them is the _____ that has taken place.
    a. development
    b. reconstruction
    c. deforestation
    d. forestation
    e. metamorphsis

22. The United States Agency for International Development (AID) in Haiti invited anthropologist _____ to develop an alternative approach to reforestation of Haiti.
    a. Richard N. Lerner
    b. Edward C. Green
    c. Harald Prins
    d. William L. Ury
    e. Gerald F. Murray

Answers to multiple-choice practice questions

1. d	7. e	13. b	19. c
2. a	8. a	14. e	20. b
3. e	9. d	15. c	21. c
4. b	10. a	16. c	22. e
5. b	11. b	17. d	
6. e	12. e	18. d	

True/False Practice

1. In case after case, the scenario is revealed in which violent acts against Brazil's indigenous peoples are never brought to justice.

2. In Brazil today, the judicial process in cases involving indigenous peoples has not gotten further than determining where the trial will be held.

3. Brazil's indigenous peoples have shown that they are unable to resist or adapt to demands imposed upon them from outside.

4. Brazilian society has shown that it is capable of overcoming two of its deepest internal conflicts: racism and the lack of punishment for those guilty of crimes against indigenous people (impunity).

5. Brazil's indigenous peoples have shown that they are not merely "remnants" of a once great past, but are fully capable of forging viable models for their future.

6. The anthropologically conceived and implemented agroforestry project in Haiti turned out to be reasonably successful.

Answers to true/false practice questions

1. T	3. F	5. T
2. T	4. F	6. T

Practice Matching

Match the culture with its characteristic.

1. _____ Skolt Lapps

2. _____ Shuar

3. _____ Wauja

4. _____ Iranians

5. _____ Tasmanians

a. Established an Islamic government after a successful religious revitalization.

b. An Amazonian people who mobilized to protect their native lands

c. Native Americans of Ecuador who formed a federation to protect their interests

d. Arctic Scandinavians whose society was radically changed by the introduction of snowmobiles

e. Indigenous people off the coast of Australia who were wiped out by Europeans

Answers to practice matching

1. d   2. c   3. b   4. a   5. e

Practice Essays

1. Describe the impact of modernization on Skolt Lapps, Shuar Indians, and Wauja.

2. In what ways can the rising tide of Islamic fundamentalism in the Middle East and other areas of the world be seen as a revitalization movement? Are there other terms from the chapter that could apply to this phenomenon? What might anthropology contribute to our understanding of such movements?

3. The violence that occurred on Indian Day in Brazil 1997 brought to the surface old problems and wounds that have never healed. Identify and discuss these old problems and wounds that still exist in Brazilian society.

4. Statistics gathered by the Indigenous Missionary Council show that not only is there an increase in violence against Brazil's indigenous people, but also in the kinds of aggression committed against them. Identify the new forms of aggression against the indigenous peoples of Brazil. How are these cases represented and reported in the national press and how are they dealt with by authorities? Are there patterns in the violence that characterize Indian/white relations?

5. How and why did the deforestation of Haiti come about? Describe and explain.

6. Describe the anthropologist's alternative approach to reforestation in Haiti. How did he arrive at this alternative approach?

Chapter 27
Anthropology and the Future

Synopsis

In this concluding chapter the text considers the role of anthropological knowledge in facing the world of the future.

What You Should Learn From This Chapter

1. Understand the contribution anthropology can make in planning for humanity's future.
2. Understand what a one-world culture is and the feasibility of such a system.
3. Consider the problems facing humankind and some possible avenues of solution.

Key Terms

cultural pluralism

structural violence

replacement reproduction

one-world culture

ethnic resurgence

global apartheid

"culture of discontent"

Review Questions

1. What shortcomings are evident in future-oriented literature?

2. What makes anthropologists uniquely suited to contribute to planning for the future?

3. Can the globe today be described as a "one-world culture"?

4. Why are predictions of a politically integrated world probably incorrect?

5. Give an example of how misunderstandings might actually increase in a one-world culture.

6. Give some contemporary examples of ethnic resurgence.

7. How does the concept of ethnocentrism interfere with cultural pluralism?

8. In what way is the world system one of "global apartheid"?

9. Provide examples of structural violence.

10. What is thought to be the immediate cause of world hunger? Provide examples.

11. Why is the suggestion that countries adopt agricultural practices similar to the United States not necessarily sound advice?

12. What is meant by the "exploitative world view"?

Fill-in-the-Blank

1. Anthropologists try to be _____, meaning they take into account many interacting factors to understand the functioning of the complex whole.

2. Anthropologists have a _____, meaning they take a long-term view of things.

3. Over the past five thousand years, political units have grown steadily _____ in size and _____ in number.

4. All large states have a tendency to _____.

5. There are about _____ recognized states in the world today, but three to five thousand national groups.

6. An important force for global unity are the _____ corporations that cut across national boundaries.

7. The separation of whites and blacks in South Africa under the domination of the white minority was a system called _____.

8. About _____ of the population of the world is nonwhite.

9. A great deal of the violence in the world is not due to the unique and personal decisions of individuals but to social, political, and economic conditions; this is referred to as _____ violence.

10. The population of the world today is about _____.

11. The cause of world hunger is not so much the ability to produce food but the ability to _____ it effectively.

12. _____ rain, caused in part by smokestack gases, is causing damage to lakes, forests, and groundwater.

13. All civilizations have an _____ world view that tends to promote ecologically unsound cultural practices.

14. Replacement reproduction refers to a rate of reproduction in which a couple have no more than _____children.

Multiple-Choice Practice Questions

1. Most people plan for the future by looking at trends in
   a. ancient history.
   b. hemlines.
   c. third-world countries.
   d. food supplies.
   e. recent history.

2. Anthropologists are trained to develop effective predictions of the future because they are
   a. have an awareness of cultural relativity.
   b. good at seeing how parts fit together into a large whole.
   c. trained to have an evolutionary perspective.
   d. able to see short-term trends in long-term perspective.
   e. All of the above

3. Over the past five thousand years, political units have
   a. grown steadily smaller in size.
   b. grown steadily larger in size and fewer in number.
   c. eliminated multinational corporations.
   d. promoted individual freedoms.
   e. eliminated slavery.

4. Multinational corporations
   a. have been widespread in Western culture since medieval times.
   b. were very common during the colonial period.
   c. have become a major force in the world today since the 1950s.
   d. have been disintegrating since the 1950s.
   e. promote relativistic rather than ethnocentric ideas.

5. Which of the following expresses the NEGATIVE consequences of multinational corporations on the international and domestic scenes?
   a. Multinational corporations cross-cut nations and thus achieve a global unity.
   b. Multinational corporations have become a major force in the world since the 1950s.
   c. Multinational corporations have become so powerful that they have been able to influence government decisions so that they benefit the company rather than the people.
   d. Multinational corporations are products of the technological revolution.
   e. They have developed sophisticated data-processing techniques that enable them to keep track of worldwide operations.

6. Cultural pluralism
   a. may constitute a temporary stage in a process of integration into a single melting-pot culture.
   b. implies the absence of bigotry and racism.
   c. implies respect for the cultural traditions of other peoples.
   d. may result from conquest or from several culturally distinct groups occupying an area that eventually becomes unified as a larger political entity.
   e. All of the above

7. Which of the following represent the NEGATIVE consequences of ethnocentrism?
   a. By believing that another culture is inferior to yours, you can, with a sense of righteousness, destroy its temples, cottage industry, polygynous practices, and so on in order to bring it into line with your culture's standards of appropriate behavior and belief.
   b. Ethnocentrism confers a sense of pride in and loyalty to one's own cultural traditions.
   c. Ethnocentrism provides a feeling of psychological gratification that one is living the right kind of life.
   d. Ethnocentrism contributes to a sense of personal worth.
   e. Ethnocentrism strengthens social solidarity.

8. "Global apartheid" refers to
   a. the prediction that in the future, South Africa will dominate the world economy.
   b. the fact that whites, although they make up only one-third of the world's population today, have greater access to the world's resources.
   c. the fact that nonwhites suffer a disproportionate share of the world's problems of hunger, pollution, and overpopulation and have a much greater chance of dying a violent death than do whites.
   d. the fact that the structure of world society is very similar to that of South Africa.
   e. All of the above except *a*

9. _____ is violence produced by social, political, and economic structures rather than by the unique and personal decisions of individuals.
   a. Torture
   b. Modernization
   c. Structural violence
   d. Insanity
   e. Religion

10. The change from subsistence farming to cash crops
    a. enables farmers to enlarge their holdings and feed their families more effectively.
    b. results in the relocation of subsistence farmers to urban areas or to lands ecologically unfit for farming.
    c. leads to the decline of multinational corporations.
    d. supports cultural pluralism.
    e. leads to revitalization.

11. The main reason an Asian wet-rice farmer might choose not to adopt North American techniques of intensive agriculture is because
    a. he or she cannot afford to buy the chemical products typically used in this type of agriculture.
    b. the North American method requires at least eight calories of energy to be expended for every calorie produced, whereas the wet-rice farmer produces three hundred calories for every calorie he or she invests.
    c. the North American method produces toxic substances that destroy delicate ecological balances.
    d. he or she predicts that the North American method, while successful for a short period of time, is sowing the seeds of its own destruction.
    e. All of the above

12. Pollution, although a worldwide consequence of certain agricultural and industrial activities, is more of a problem in _____ because chemicals that may be banned in richer nations can be used more easily.
    a. poor countries.
    b. industrialized countries.
    c. arctic countries.
    d. Mediterranean countries.
    e. ocean areas.

13. If a country achieves "replacement reproduction," this means that
    a. people produce only enough children to replace themselves when they die.
    b. each reproductive couple has no more children.
    c. its population will immediately stop growing.
    d. its population will continue to grow for another fifty years.
    e. every other generation can have children.

14. The most extreme form of female genital mutilation is
    a. female circumcision.
    b. breast implantation.
    c. infibulation.
    d. appendectomy.
    e. tonsillectomy.

Answers to multiple choice practice questions

1. e	5. c	9. c	13. a
2. e	6. e	10. b	14. c
3. b	7. a	11. a	
4. c	8. e	12. a	

True/False Practice Questions

1. Multinational corporations have constituted a strong force for global unity.

2. Structural violence refers to violence produced by social, political, and economic structures rather than by the unique and personal decisions of individuals.

3. The change from subsistence farming to cash crops leads to economic improvements in countries that made the change.

4. Modernization refers to a situation in which groups with different ways of acting and thinking can interact socially with mutual respect.

5. The question of choice is central to the story of how medicine and business generate controlling processes in the shaping of women's bodies.

6. Sudanese and other African women, North American women, and others experience body mutilation as part of engendering rites.

7. Cosmetic surgery in the United States is necessary to the patient's psychological health.

8. Social surveys indicate that, to the extent that women internalize the social imperative that they can enhance their lives by enhancing their breasts, they feel they are making the decision on their own.

9. In the Sudan, the young girl is told that circumcision and infibulation are done to her not for her.

10. According to Linda Coco, the operation on the female breast in North America does NOT hold the same symbolism and expression of cultural mandate as does infibulation in Sudan.

11. The interest of Cultural Survival, Inc. is to preserve indigenous cultures in their original pristine condition so that they will be there to study and to serve as living museum exhibits.

12. Much remains to be done to secure the survival of indigenous peoples in all parts of the world.

Answers to true/false practice questions

1. T	5. T	9. F
2. T	6. T	10. F
3. F	7. T	11. F
4. F	8. T	12. T

Practice Essay

1. The effort to reduce population growth faces enormous cultural obstacles. Illustrate this by describing Chinese efforts to promote one-child families, and consider whether Western planners should attempt to encourage similar efforts in the Islamic world, where birth control is prohibited on religious grounds. Where does appropriate global planning run up against the charge of ethnocentrism or cultural imperialism?

2. One of the most heated debates arising from the public health concern over breast implants is whether the recipient's decision is voluntary or whether control is disguised as free will. Explain what is meant by this.

3. What is the main interest of the advocacy group Cultural Survival, Inc.? Describe what they are trying to do for indigenous peoples. What are some of their success stories?